THE GRAYWOLF ANNUAL THREE

ESSAYS, MEMOIRS & REFLECTIONS

THE GRAYWOLF ANNUAL THREE: ESSAYS, MEMOIRS & REFLECTIONS

EDITED BY SCOTT WALKER

GRAYWOLF PRESS : SAINT PAUL

The essays collected in this *Graywolf Annual* appeared previously in the publications noted below. Most of John Haines's essay, "Shadows," appears here for the first time. Patricia Hampl's essay also receives its first publication here; it is part of a long work-in-progress.

John Berger's "Her Secrets" was first published in *The Three-Penny Review*. Copyright © 1986 by John Berger.

Annie Dillard's "Singing with the Fundamentalists" first appeared in *The Yale Review*. Copyright © 1985 by Annie Dillard.

"Reflections on the Death of John Gardner," by Terrence Des Pres, also received first publication in *The Yale Review*. Copyright © 1983 by Terrence Des Pres.

Phillip Moffitt's "The Power of One Woman" was published in *Esquire*. Copyright © 1986 by Phillip Moffitt.

"Growing Up Game," Brenda Peterson's essay, was first published in Seattle's *The Weekly*. Copyright © 1986 by Brenda Peterson.

"Story at Anaktuvuk Pass" first appeared in *Harper's* magazine. Copyright © 1985 by Barry Lopez.

Richard Ford's "The Three Kings" was first published in *Esquire*. Copyright © 1985 by Richard Ford.

"Looking for a Lost Dog" first appeared in *New Age Journal*. Copyright © 1986 by Gretel Ehrlich.

Suzannah Lessard's essay first appeared in "Talk of the Town" in *The New Yorker*. Copyright © 1985 by Suzannah Lessard.

"The Snap Election" appeared, as part one of a three-part article, in *Granta*. Copyright © 1986 by James Fenton.

David Quammen's "The Same River Twice" appeared as one of his regular columns in *Outside* magazine. Copyright © 1986 by David Quammen.

"Drinking and Driving" by William Kittredge appears here in a much revised version of the essay that was originally published in *Outside* and *Montana: The Magazine of Western History*. Copyright © 1986 by William Kittredge.

ISBN 0-915308-88-6 / ISSN 0743-7471
Library of Congress Catalog Card Number 86-81785
First printing, 1986
Designed by Tree Swenson
Baskerville type set by Walker & Swenson

Publication of this book is made possible in part by a generous donation from The Bush Foundation, and a grant from the Literature Program of the National Endowment for the Arts. Graywolf Press is a member organization of United Arts.

Published by Graywolf Press, Post Office Box 75006
Saint Paul, Minnesota 55175.

CONTENTS

✖

Foreword

v

John Berger

HER SECRETS

3

Annie Dillard

SINGING WITH
THE FUNDAMENTALISTS

9

Terrence Des Pres

REFLECTIONS ON THE DEATH
OF JOHN GARDNER

23

Phillip Moffitt

THE POWER OF ONE WOMAN

47

Brenda Peterson

GROWING UP GAME

55

Barry Lopez

STORY AT ANAKTUVUK PASS

59

Richard Ford

THE THREE KINGS

67

Gretel Ehrlich

LOOKING FOR A LOST DOG

89

Suzannah Lessard

from THE TALK OF THE TOWN

93

James Fenton

THE SNAP ELECTION

99

David Quammen

THE SAME RIVER TWICE

135

John Haines

SHADOWS

143

Patricia Hampl

PARISH STREETS

155

William Kittredge

DRINKING & DRIVING

167

FOREWORD

AFTER A TIME, some of us learn (and some more slowly than others), that life comes down to some simple things. How we love, how alert we are, how curious we are. Love, attention, curiosity. Layer by layer, we discover and peel away superstitions, fantasies, projections, levels of hate and anger and confusion, in order to experience the people and the life around us – and our life in the world – as directly and clearly as possible.

One way we learn this lesson is by listening to others tell us true stories of their own struggles to come to a way of understanding. We are fascinated by their mistakes, their humility, their ability to laugh at themselves, and their slow evolution of perspective. It is sometimes comforting to know that others seem to fail as often and as oddly as we do. It is comforting, too, to know that others, more articulate than we are, evolve, along with that mysterious perspective, a profound sense of forgiveness, of both themselves and others. And it is even more comforting to have such stories told to us with *style*, the way a writer has found to an individual expression of a personal truth.

When William Kittredge writes, in his essay titled "Drinking and Driving," "Deep in the far heart of my upbringing, a crew of us 16-year-old lads were driven crazy with ill-defined midsummer sadness by the damp, sour-smelling sweetness of nighttime alfalfa fields, an infinity of stars and moonglow, and no girlfriends whatsoever. Frogs croaked in the lonesome swamp…," there occurs in some readers a rumbling laughter, a weeping that seems to come from some far place, and a satisfying sense of affirmation. We have been there. We are there still, in ways that are mysterious and comforting.

Similarly, when Annie Dillard has the compassion and sense of adventure to join the Fundamentalists singing by the fountain, as well as the audacity to tell about it, we are encouraged; our curiosity and compassion are revived.

In recent years, we have been pleased to note the renaissance of the short story. More and more writers have turned to the short story as a means of expression, and the form has been explored with great liveliness. We devoted the first two *Graywolf Annuals* to anthologies of short stories and were pleased (and somewhat amazed) that our efforts were received by readers with such enthusiasm.

We sense that a similar renaissance of interest is occurring in nonfiction prose as more and more writers turn to the essay or memoir as a fitting way to tell a more directly personal sort of truth than might be told in fiction. More magazines allow the personal essay space once reserved for informational articles. We are pleased by the idea of a renewal of interest in the essay, and the opportunity to broaden the audience for this sort of writing appeals to us as publishers.

And so we offer *The Graywolf Annual Three: Essays, Memoirs & Reflections*, an informal and lively anthology which demonstrates a dozen or so ways that essays can be personal: from literary memoir to firsthand political reportage to remembrances of family life.

Reading a personal essay provides a unique opportunity to communicate with a stranger by way of the relaxed intimacy usually reserved for close friends and members of the family. We are blessed to have an opportunity to extend our family by way of reading good prose.

SCOTT WALKER
September 1986

THE GRAYWOLF ANNUAL THREE

ESSAYS, MEMOIRS & REFLECTIONS

JOHN BERGER

✖

Her Secrets

FOR KATYA

From the age of five or six I was worried about the death of my parents. The inevitability of death was one of the first things I learnt about the world on my own. Nobody else spoke of it yet the signs were so clear.

Every time I went to bed – and in this I am sure I was like millions of other children – the fear that one or both my parents might die in the night touched the nape of my neck with its finger. Such a fear has, I believe, little to do with a particular psychological climate and a great deal to do with nightfall. Yet since it was impossible to say: You won't die in the night, will you? (when Grandmother died, I was told she had gone to have a rest, or – this was from my uncle who was more outspoken – that she had passed over), since I couldn't ask the real question and I sought a reassurance, I invented – like millions before me – the euphemism: See you in the morning! To which either my father or mother, who had come to turn out the light in my bedroom, would reply: See you in the morning, John.

After their footsteps had died away, I would try for as long as possible not to lift my head from the pillow so that the last words spoken remained, trapped like fish in a rock-pool at low tide, between my pillow and ear. The implicit promise of the words was also a protection against the dark. The words promised that I would not (yet) be alone.

Now I'm no longer usually frightened by the dark and my father died ten years ago and my mother a month ago at the age of ninety-three. It would be a natural moment to write an autobiography. My version of my life can no longer hurt either of them. And the book, when finished, would be there, a little like a parent. Autobiography begins with a sense of being alone. It is an orphan form. Yet I have no wish to do so. All that interests me about my past life are the common moments. The moments – which if I relate them well enough – will join countless others lived by people I do not personally know.

Six weeks ago my mother asked me to come and see her; it would be the last time, she said. A few days later, on the morning of my birthday, she believed she was dying. Open the curtains, she asked my brother, so I can see the trees. In fact, she died the following week.

On my birthdays as a child, it was my father rather than she who gave me memorable presents. She was too thrifty. Her moments of generosity were at the table, offering what she had bought and prepared and cooked and served to whoever came into the house. Otherwise she was thrifty. Nor did she ever explain. She was secretive, she kept things to herself. Not for her own pleasure, but because the world would not forgive spontaneity, the world was mean. I must make that clearer. She didn't believe life was mean – it was generous – but she had learnt from her own childhood that survival was hard. She was the opposite of quixotic – for she was not born a knight and her father was a warehouse foreman in Lambeth. She pursed her lips together, knitted her brows as she calculated and thought things out and carried on with an unspoken determination. She never asked favors of anyone. Nothing shocked her. From whatever she saw, she just drew the necessary conclusions so as to survive and to be dependent on nobody. If I were Æsop, I would say that in her prudence and persistence my mother resembled the agouti. (I once wrote about an agouti in the London zoo, but I did not then realize why the animal so touched me.) In my adult life, the only occasions on which we shouted at each other were when she estimated I was being quixotic.

When I was in my thirties she told me for the first time that, ever since I was born, she had hoped I would be a writer. The writers she admired when young were Bernard Shaw, J. M. Barrie, Compton Mackenzie, Warwick Deeping, E. M. Dell. The only painter she really admired was Turner – perhaps because of her childhood on the banks of the Thames.

Most of my books she didn't read. Either because they dealt with subjects which were alien to her or because – under the protective influence of my father – she believed they might upset her. Why suffer surprise from something which, left unopened, gives you pleasure? My being a writer was unqualified for her by what I wrote. To be a writer was to be able to see to the horizon where, anyway, nothing is ever very distinct and all questions are open. Literature had little to do with the writer's vocation as she saw it. It was only a by-product. A writer was a person familiar with the secrets. Perhaps in the end she didn't read my books so that they should remain more secret.

If her hopes of my becoming a writer – and she said they began on the night after I was delivered – were eventually realized, it was not because there were many books in our house (there were few) but because there was so much that was unsaid, so much that I had to discover the existence of on my own at an early age: death, poverty, pain (in others), sexuality...

These things were there to be discovered within the house or from its windows – until I left for good, more or less prepared for the outside world, at the age of eight. My mother never spoke of these things. She didn't hide the fact that she was aware of them. For her, however, they were wrapped secrets, to be lived with, but never to be mentioned or opened. Superficially this was a question of gentility, but profoundly, of a respect, a secret loyalty to the enigmatic. My rough and ready preparation for the world did not include a single explanation – it simply consisted of the principle that events carried more weight than the self.

Thus, she taught me very little – at least in the usual sense of the term: she a teacher about life, I a learner. By imitating her gestures I learnt how to roast meat in the oven, how to clean celery, how to cook rice, how to choose vegetables in a market. As a young woman she had been a vegetarian. Then she gave it up because she did not want to influence us children. Why were you a vegetarian? I once asked her, eating my Sunday roast, much later when I was first working as a journalist. Because I'm against killing. She would say no more. Either I understood or I didn't. There was nothing more to be said.

In time – and I understand this only now writing these pages – I chose to visit abattoirs in different cities of the world and to become something of an expert concerning the subject. The unspoken, the unfaceable beckoned me. I followed. Into the abattoirs and, differently, into many other places and situations.

The last, the largest and the most personally prepared wrapped secret was her own death. Of course I was not the only witness. Of those close to her, I was maybe the most removed, the most remote. But she knew, I think, with confidence that I would pursue the matter. She knew that if anybody can be at home with what is kept a secret, it was me, because I was her son whom she hoped would become a writer.

The clinical history of her illness is a different story about which she herself was totally uncurious. Sufficient to say that with the help of drugs she was not in pain, and that, thanks to my brother and sister-in-law who arranged everything for her, she was not subjected to all the mechanical ingenuity of aids for the artificial prolongation of life.

Of how many deaths – though never till now of my own mother's – have I written? Truly we writers are the secretaries of death.

She lay in bed, propped up by pillows, her head fallen forward, as if asleep.

I shut my eyes, she said, I like to shut my eyes and think. I don't sleep though. If I slept now, I wouldn't sleep at night.

What do you think about?

She screwed up her eyes which were gimlet sharp and looked at me, twinkling, as if I'd never, not even as a small child, asked such a stupid question.

Are you working hard? What are you writing?

A play, I answered.

The last time I went to the theater I didn't understand a thing, she said. It's not my hearing that's bad though.

Perhaps the play was obscure, I suggested.

She opened her eyes again. The body has closed shop, she announced. Nothing, nothing at all from here down. She placed a hand on her neck. It's a good thing, make no mistake about it, John, it makes the waiting easier.

On her bedside table was a tin of handcream. I started to massage her left hand.

Do you remember a photograph I once took of your hands? Working hands, you said.

No, I don't.

Would you like some more photos on your table? Katya, her granddaughter, asked her.

She smiled at Katya and shook her head, her voice very slightly broken by a laugh. It would be *so* difficult, so difficult, wouldn't it, to choose.

She turned towards me. What exactly are you doing?

I'm massaging your hand. It's meant to be pleasurable.

To tell you the truth, dear, it doesn't make much difference. What plane are you taking back?

I mumbled, took her other hand.

You are all worried, she said, especially when there are several of you. I'm not. Maureen asked me the other day whether I wanted to be cremated or buried. Doesn't make one iota of difference to me. How could it? She shut her eyes to think.

For the first time in her life and in mine, she could openly place the wrapped enigma between us. She didn't watch me watching it, for we had the habits of a lifetime. Openly she knew that at that moment her faith in a secret was bound to be stronger than any faith of mine in facts. With her eyes still shut, she fingered the Arab necklace I'd attached round her neck with a charm against the evil eye. I'd given her the necklace a few hours before. Perhaps for the first time I had offered her a secret and now her hand kept looking for it.

She opened her eyes. What time is it?

Quarter to four.

It's not very interesting talking to me, you know. I don't have any ideas any more. I've had a good life. Why don't you take a walk?

Katya stayed with her.

When you are very old, she told Katya confidentially, there's one thing that's very very difficult — it's very difficult to persuade other people that you're happy.

She let her head go back onto the pillow. As I came back in, she smiled.

In her right hand she held a crumpled paper handkerchief. With it she dabbed from time to time the corner of her mouth when she felt there was the slightest excess of spittle there. The gesture was reminiscent of one with which, many years before, she used to wipe her mouth after drinking Earl Grey tea and eating watercress sandwiches. Meanwhile with her left hand she fingered the necklace, cushioned on her forgotten bosom.

Love, my mother had the habit of saying, is the only thing that counts in this world. Real love, she would add, to avoid any factitious misunderstanding. But apart from that simple adjective, she never added anything more.

ANNIE DILLARD

✠

Singing with the Fundamentalists

I<small>T IS EARLY SPRING</small>. I have a temporary office at a state university on the West Coast. The office is on the third floor. It looks down on the Square, the enormous open courtyard at the center of campus. From my desk I see hundreds of people moving between classes. There is a large circular fountain in the Square's center.

Early one morning, on the first day of spring quarter, I hear singing. A pack of students has gathered at the fountain. They are singing something which, at this distance, and through the heavy window, sounds good.

I know who these singing students are: they are the Fundamentalists. This campus has a lot of them. Mornings they sing on the Square; it is their only perceptible activity. What are they singing? Whatever it is, I want to join them, for I like to sing; whatever it is, I want to take my stand with them, for I am drawn to their very absurdity, their innocent indifference to what people think. My colleagues and students here, and my friends everywhere, dislike and fear Christian fundamentalists. You may never have met such people, but you've heard what they do: they pile up money, vote in blocs, and elect right-wing crazies; they censor books; they carry handguns; they fight fluoride in the drinking water and evolution in the schools; probably they would lynch people if they could get away with it. I'm not sure my friends are correct. I close my pen and join the singers on the Square.

There is a clapping song in progress. I have to concentrate to follow it:

> Come on, rejoice,
> And let your heart sing,
> Come on, rejoice,
> Give praise to the king.
> Singing alleluia –
> He is the king of kings;
> Singing alleluia –
> He is the king of kings.

Two song leaders are standing on the broad rim of the fountain; the water is splashing just behind them. The boy is short, hard-faced, with a moustache. He bangs his guitar with the backs of his fingers. The blonde girl, who leads the clapping, is bouncy; she wears a bit of make-up. Both are wearing blue jeans.

The students beside me are wearing blue jeans too – and athletic jerseys, parkas, football jackets, turtlenecks, and hiking shoes or jogging shoes. They all have canvas or nylon book bags. They look like any random batch of seventy or eighty students at this university. They are grubby or scrubbed, mostly scrubbed; they are tall, fair, or red-headed in large proportions. Their parents are white-collar workers, blue-collar workers, farmers, loggers, orchardists, merchants, fishermen; their names are, I'll bet, Olsen, Jensen, Seversen, Hansen, Klokker, Sigurdsen.

Despite the vigor of the clapping song, no one seems to be giving it much effort. And no one looks at anyone else; there are no sentimental glances and smiles, no glances even of recognition. These kids don't seem to know each other. We stand at the fountain's side, out on the broad, bricked Square in front of the science building, and sing the clapping song through three times.

It is quarter to nine in the morning. Hundreds of people are crossing the Square. These passersby — faculty, staff, students — pay very little attention to us; this morning singing has gone on for years. Most of them look at us directly, then ignore us, for there is nothing to see: no animal sacrifices, no lynchings, no collection plate for Jesse Helms, no seizures, snake handling, healing, or glossolalia. There is barely anything to hear. I suspect the people glance at us to learn if we are really singing: how could so many people make so little sound? My fellow singers, who ignore each other, certainly ignore passersby as well. Within a week, most of them will have their eyes closed anyway.

We move directly to another song, a slower one.

> He is my peace
> Who has broken down every wall;
> He is my peace,
> He is my peace.
>
> Cast all your cares on him,
> For he careth for you — oo — oo
> He is my peace,
> He is my peace.

I am paying strict attention to the song leaders, for I am singing at the top of my lungs and I've never heard any of these songs before. They are not the old American low-church Protestant hymns; they are not the old European high-church Protestant hymns. These hymns seem to have been written just yesterday, apparently by the same people who put out lyrical Christian greeting cards and bookmarks.

"Where do these songs come from?" I ask a girl standing next to me. She seems appalled to be addressed at all, and startled by the question. "They're from the praise albums!" she explains, and moves away.

The songs' melodies run dominant, subdominant, dominant, tonic, dominant. The pace is slow, about the pace of "Tell

Laura I Love Her," and with that song's quavering, long notes. The lyrics are simple and repetitive; there are very few of them to which a devout Jew or Mohammedan could not give whole-hearted assent. These songs are similar to the things Catholics sing in church these days. I don't know if any studies have been done to correlate the introduction of contemporary songs into Catholic churches with those churches' decline in membership, or with the phenomenon of Catholic converts' applying to en-ter cloistered monasteries directly, without passing through parish churches.

> I'm set free to worship,
> I'm set free to praise him,
> I'm set free to dance before the Lord...

At nine o'clock sharp we quit and scatter. I hear a few quiet "see you"s. Mostly the students leave quickly, as if they didn't want to be seen. The Square empties.

THE NEXT DAY we show up again, at twenty to nine. The same two leaders stand on the fountain's rim; the fountain is pouring down behind them.

After the first song, the boy with the moustache hollers, "Move on up! Some of you guys aren't paying attention back there! You're talking to each other. I want you to concentrate!" The students laugh, embarrassed for him. He sounds like a teacher. No one moves. The girl breaks into the next song, which we join at once:

> In my life, Lord,
> Be glorified, be glorified, be glorified;
> In my life, Lord,
> Be glorified, be glorified, today.

At the end of this singularly monotonous verse, which is strain-ing my tolerance for singing virtually anything, the boy with the moustache startles me by shouting, "Classes!"

At once, without skipping a beat, we sing, "In my classes, Lord, be glorified, be glorified…" I give fleet thought to the class I'm teaching this afternoon. We're reading a little "Talk of the Town" piece called "Eggbag," about a cat in a magic store on Eighth Avenue. "Relationships!" the boy calls. The students seem to sing "In my relationships, Lord," more easily than they sang "classes." They seemed embarrassed by "classes." In fact, to my fascination, they seem embarrassed by almost everything. Why are they here? I will sing with the Fundamentalists every weekday morning all spring; I will decide, tentatively, that they come pretty much for the same reasons I do: each has a private relationship with "the Lord" and will put up with a lot of junk for it.

I HAVE TAUGHT some Fundamentalist students here, and know a bit of what they think. They are college students above all, worried about their love lives, their grades, and finding jobs. Some support moderate Democrats; some support moderate Republicans. Like their classmates, most support nuclear freeze, ERA, and an end to the draft. I believe they are divided on abortion and busing. They are not particularly political. They read *Christianity Today* and *Campus Life* and *Eternity* – moderate, sensible magazines, I think; they read a lot of C. S. Lewis. (One such student, who seemed perfectly tolerant of me and my shoddy Christianity, introduced me to C. S. Lewis's critical book on Charles Williams.) They read the Bible. I think they all "believe in" organic evolution. The main thing about them is this: there isn't any "them." Their views vary. They don't know each other.

Their common Christianity puts them, if anywhere, to the left of their classmates. I believe they also tend to be more able than their classmates to think well in the abstract, and also to recognize the complexity of moral issues. But I may be wrong.

IN 1980, the media were certainly wrong about television evangelists. Printed estimates of Jerry Falwell's television audience ranged from 18 million to 30 million people. In fact, according to Arbitron's actual counts, fewer than 1.5 million people were watching Falwell. And, according to an Emory University study, those who did watch television evangelists didn't necessarily vote with them. Emory University sociologist G. Melton Mobley reports, "When that message turns political, they cut it off." Analysis of the 1982 off-year election turned up no Fundamentalist bloc voting. The media were wrong, but no one printed retractions.

The media were wrong, too, in a tendency to identify all fundamentalist Christians with Falwell and his ilk, and to attribute to them, across the board, conservative views.

Someone has sent me two recent issues of *Eternity: The Evangelical Monthly*. One lead article criticizes a television preacher for saying that the United States had never used military might to take land from another nation. The same article censures Newspeak, saying that government rhetoric would have us believe in a "clean bomb," would have us believe that we "defend" America by invading foreign soil, and would have us believe that the dictatorships we support are "democracies." "When the President of the United States says that one reason to support defense spending is because it creates jobs," this lead article says, "a little bit of *1984* begins to surface." Another article criticizes a "heavy-handed" opinion of Jerry Falwell Ministries – in this case a broadside attack on artificial insemination, surrogate motherhood, and lesbian motherhood. Browsing through *Eternity*, I find a double crosstic. I find an intelligent, analytical, and enthusiastic review of the new London Philharmonic recording of Mahler's second symphony – a review which stresses the "glorious truth" of the Jewish composer's magnificent work, and cites its recent performance in Jerusalem to celebrate the recapture of the Western Wall following the Six Day War. Surely, the evangelical Christians who read this magazine are not book-burners. If by chance they vote with the magazine's editors, then it looks to me as if they vote with the

American Civil Liberties Union and Americans for Democratic Action.

Every few years some bold and sincere Christian student at this university disagrees with a professor in class – usually about the professor's out-of-hand dismissal of Christianity. Members of the faculty, outraged, repeat the stories of these rare and uneven encounters for years on end, as if to prove that the crazies are everywhere, and gaining ground. The notion is, apparently, that these kids can't think for themselves. Or they wouldn't disagree.

Now AGAIN the moustached leader asks us to move up. There is no harangue, so we move up. (This will be a theme all spring. The leaders want us closer together. Our instinct is to stand alone.) From behind the tall fountain comes a wind; on several gusts we get sprayed. No one seems to notice.

We have time for one more song. The leader, perhaps sensing that no one likes him, blunders on. "I want you to pray this one through," he says. "We have a lot of people here from a lot of different fellowships, but we're all one body. Amen?" They don't like it. He gets a few polite Amens. We sing:

> Bind us together, Lord,
> With a bond that can't be broken;
> Bind us together, Lord,
> With love.

Everyone seems to be in a remarkably foul mood today. We don't like this song. There is no one here under seventeen, and, I think, no one here who believes that love is a bond that can't be broken. We sing the song through three times; then it is time to go.

The leader calls after our retreating backs, "Hey, have a good day! Praise Him all day!" The kids around me roll up their eyes privately. Some groan; all flee.

THE NEXT MORNING is very cold. I am here early. Two girls are talking on the fountain's rim; one is part Indian. She says, "I've got all the Old Testament, but I can't get the New. I screw up the New." She takes a breath and rattles off a long list, ending with "Jonah, Micah, Nahum, Habakkuk, Zephaniah, Haggai, Zechariah, Malachi." The other girl produces a slow, sarcastic applause. I ask one of the girls to help me with the words to a song. She is agreeable, but says, "I'm sorry, I can't. I just became a Christian this year, so I don't know all the words yet."

The others are coming; we stand and separate. The boy with the moustache is gone, replaced by a big, serious fellow in a green down jacket. The bouncy girl is back with her guitar; she's wearing a skirt and wool knee socks. We begin, without any preamble, by singing a song that has so few words that we actually stretch one syllable over eleven separate notes. Then we sing a song in which the men sing one phrase and the women echo it. Everyone seems to know just what to do. In the context of our vapid songs, the lyrics of this one are extraordinary:

> I was nothing before you found me.
> Heartache! Broken people! Ruined lives
> Is why you died on Calvary.

The last line rises in a regular series of half-notes. Now at last some people are actually singing; they throw some breath into the business. There is a seriousness and urgency to it: "Heartache! Broken people! Ruined lives...I was nothing."

We don't look like nothing. We look like a bunch of students of every stripe, ill-shaven or well-shaven, dressed up or down, but dressed warmly against the cold: jeans and parkas, jeans and heavy sweaters, jeans and scarves and blow-dried hair. We look ordinary. But I think, quite on my own, that we are here because we know this business of nothingness, brokenness, and ruination. We sing this song over and over.

Something catches my eye. Behind us, up in the science

building, professors are standing alone at opened windows.

The long brick science building has three upper floors of faculty offices, thirty-two windows. At one window stands a bearded man, about forty; his opening his window is what caught my eye. He stands full in the open window, his hands on his hips, his head cocked down toward the fountain. He is drawn to look, as I was drawn to come. Up on the building's top floor, at the far right window, there is another: an Asian-American professor, wearing a white shirt, is sitting with one hip on his desk, looking out and down. In the middle of the row of windows, another one, an old professor in a checked shirt, stands sideways to the opened window, stands stock-still, his long, old ear to the air. Now another window cranks open, another professor – or maybe a graduate student – leans out, his hands on the sill.

We are all singing, and I am watching these five still men, my colleagues, whose office doors are surely shut – for that is the custom here: five of them alone in their offices in the science building who have opened their windows on this very cold morning, who motionless hear the Fundamentalists sing, utterly unknown to each other.

We sing another four songs, including the clapping song, and one which repeats, "This is the day which the Lord hath made; rejoice and be glad in it." All the professors but one stay by their opened windows, figures in a frieze. When after ten minutes we break off and scatter, each cranks his window shut. Maybe they have nine o'clock classes too.

I MISS a few sessions. One morning of the following week, I rejoin the Fundamentalists on the Square. The wind is blowing from the north; it is sunny and cold. There are several new developments.

Someone has blown up rubber gloves and floated them in the fountain. I saw them yesterday afternoon from my high office window, and couldn't quite make them out: I seemed to see hands in the fountain waving from side to side, like those hands wagging on springs which people stick in the back windows of their cars. I saw these many years ago in Quito and Guayaquil, where they were a great fad long before they showed up here. The cardboard hands said, on their palms, HOLA GENTE, hello people. Some of them just said HOLA, hello, with a little wave to the universe at large, in case anybody happened to be looking. It is like our sending radio signals to planets in other galaxies: HOLA, if anyone is listening. Jolly folk, these Ecuadorians, I thought.

Now, waiting by the fountain for the singing, I see that these particular hands are long surgical gloves, yellow and white, ten of them, tied off at the cuff. They float upright and they wave, *hola, hola, hola*; they mill around like a crowd, bobbing under the fountain's spray and back again to the pool's rim, *hola*. It is a good prank. It is far too cold for the university's maintenance crew to retrieve them without turning off the fountain and putting on rubber boots.

From all around the Square, people are gathering for the singing. There is no way I can guess which kids, from among the masses crossing the Square, will veer off to the fountain. When they get here, I never recognize anybody except the leaders.

The singing begins without ado as usual, but there is something different about it. The students are growing prayerful, and they show it this morning with a peculiar gesture. I'm glad they weren't like this when I first joined them, or I never would have stayed.

Last night there was an educational television special, part of "Middletown." It was a segment called "Community of Praise," and I watched it because it was about Fundamentalists. It showed a Jesus-loving family in the Midwest; the treatment was good and complex. This family attended the prayer meetings, healing sessions, and church services of an unnamed sect — a very low-church sect, whose doctrine and culture were much more low-church than those of the kids I sing with. When the members of this sect prayed, they held their arms over their heads and raised their palms, as if to feel or receive a blessing or energy from above.

Now today on the Square there is a new serious mood. The leaders are singing with their eyes shut. I am impressed that they can bang their guitars, keep their balance, and not fall into the pool. It is the same bouncy girl and earnest boy. Their eyeballs are rolled back a bit. I look around and see that almost everyone in this crowd of eighty or so has his eyes shut and is apparently praying the words of this song or praying some other prayer.

Now as the chorus rises, as it gets louder and higher and simpler in melody –

> I exalt thee,
> I exalt thee,
> I exalt thee,
> Thou art the Lord –

then, at this moment, hands start rising. All around me, hands are going up – that tall girl, that blond boy with his head back, the red-headed boy up front, the girl with the MacDonald's jacket. Their arms rise as if pulled on strings. Some few of them have raised their arms very high over their heads and are tilting back their palms. Many, many more of them, as inconspicuously as possible, have raised their hands to the level of their chins.

What is going on? Why are these students today raising their palms in this gesture, when nobody did it last week? Is it because the leaders have set a prayerful tone this morning? Is it because this gesture always accompanies this song, just as clapping accompanies other songs? Or is it, as I suspect, that these kids watched the widely publicized documentary last night just as I did, and are adopting, or trying out, the gesture?

It is a sunny morning, and the sun is rising behind the leaders and the fountain, so those students have their heads tilted, eyes closed, and palms upraised toward the sun. I glance up at the science building and think my own prayer: thank God no one is watching this.

The leaders cannot move around much on the fountain's rim. The girl has her eyes shut; the boy opens his eyes from time to time, glances at the neck of his guitar, and closes his eyes again.

When the song is over, the hands go down, and there is some desultory chatting in the crowd, as usual: can I borrow your library card? And, as usual, nobody looks at anybody.

All our songs today are serious. There is a feudal theme to them, or a feudal analogue:

> I will eat from abundance of your household.
> I will dream beside your streams of righteousness.
>
> You are my king.
>
> Enter his gates
> with thanksgiving in your heart;
> come before his courts with praise.
>
> He is the king of kings.
>
> Thou art the Lord.

All around me, eyes are closed and hands are raised. There is no social pressure to do this, or anything else. I've never known any group to be less cohesive, imposing fewer controls. Since no one looks at anyone, and since passersby no longer look, everyone out here is inconspicuous and free. Perhaps the palm-raising has begun because the kids realize by now that they are not on display; they're praying in their closets, right out here on the Square. Over the course of the next weeks, I will learn that the palm-raising is here to stay.

The sun is rising higher. We are singing our last song. We are praying. We are alone together.

He is my peace
Who has broken down every wall...

When the song is over, the hands go down. The heads lower, the eyes open and blink. We stay still a second before we break up. We have been standing in a broad current; now we have stepped aside. We have dismantled the radar cups; we have closed the telescope's vault. Students gather their book bags and go. The two leaders step down from the fountain's rim and pack away their guitars. Everyone scatters. I am in no hurry, so I stay after everyone is gone. It is after nine o'clock, and the Square is deserted. The fountain is playing to an empty house. In the pool the cheerful hands are waving over the water, bobbing under the fountain's veil and out again in the current, *hola*.

TERRENCE DES PRES

✖

Reflections on the Death
of John Gardner

I look down past stars to a terrifying darkness. I seem to recognize the place, but it's impossible. "Accident," I whisper.
— GRENDEL

AROUND TWO in the afternoon, one of those extra-clear September days, John Gardner died in a single-vehicle accident on
a highway curve just north of Susquehanna, Pa. It was the four-
teenth of the month, 1982. Gardner was riding his '79 Harley-
Davidson, the big one called the *hog*, and when the accident happened, something – police speculate it was the stub of the bike's
handlebar – hit him very hard in the gut. Death resulted from
internal bleeding, or so the coroner determined, but in any
case Gardner never made it to the hospital. He was dead on arrival, age forty-nine, the author of twenty-eight books. Next
day, Binghamton's *Sun-Bulletin* reported that "the motorcycle,
headed north, went off the right-hand dirt shoulder, hit a
guardrail and skidded up the road into a grassy area about 20
yards past where Gardner was found." Writing later for *Boston*, a
magazine for young professionals, novelist Anne Bernays saw it
another way: "John Gardner, an experienced rider of motorcycles, drove his bike into the gravel and onto the shoulder of
Route 92…, overturning it and dying." We might almost suppose, from these different descriptions, different accidents. And
if something seems odd, some *indécidabilité radicale* as Saussure
might have said, the trouble isn't only words. Both descriptions

are inaccurate, each depends on myth, but they both say exactly what they aim to. Divergence of views isn't the problem, but rather how the accident's inherent uncertainty, which is indeed radical, can be used to take a manner of dying and make it stamp a life.

The Police Accident Report says that at an approximate speed of 50 mph, bike and rider came out of the curve and then ran off the road, then traveled along the shoulder for 87 feet, at which point, somehow back on the pavement, the motorcycle turned over on its left side. But then, rider and bike "apparently" traveled forward another 30 feet or so, and this does not seem to have been in a skid. Then the rider was off. Then the machine went on on its own, up the roadway and through a guardrail already down, falling finally on its right side, about nine feet off the asphalt. Gardner lay in the road, the Harley far away in the grass, at the edge of a wooded slope inclining downward to the Susquehanna River. So that was the accident. The description sounds clear but it isn't. If you try to imagine it you can't. In other words, nobody knows what happened. Damage to the motorcycle was moderate and the rider, of course, died. But how all this took place, on a clear dry day, at no great rate of speed, on a straight flat stretch of highway past the curve itself, is hard to see.

The motorcycle did not, as the *Sun-Bulletin* said, hit a guardrail, although it makes sense to think so; something must have caused the fatal impact. The police report suggests a slightly different, but no less incomplete, sequence of events. But no law was broken, no one else was hurt or involved; therefore the decent thing, as both police and newspaper know, is to let the dead man rest in peace. They cast no blame nor do they judge. If some definite agent caused the wreck – here is where the myth starts – let it be the bike itself. The *motorcycle* headed north. The *motorcycle* skidded, dumped its rider and went on up the road. And that is how most people, reading about it in a newspaper, would expect to see an accident like this one described. Myths arise where knowing crosses into the unknown, and so too in this case. How the bike could have crashed, then continued, then thrown its rider, then gone on by itself – it's as if the machine were its own driver. And this is also part of the myth. People who know motorcycles know that the big ones behave with a power never wholly contained. In the range of 1000 ccs, bikes begin to possess life and will of their own, or so it seems to wise riders. Men and women who ride seriously take this into account; they make a truce with the machine, and if this sounds strange to some, it would not have to Gardner. He agreed (we spoke of it more than once) that what motorcycles are about has very little to do with crazy carelessness, or with loud folly, or with the jumble of sex, speed, and heavy metal that genteel folk sometimes suppose. Respect, as if the machine had a mind of its own, is safety's first rule.

The *Sun-Bulletin* provides the best story it can, respectful, accurate in the main, then moves on to the next day's news. The police also close the case; they write it up, give it an incident number, and file it away. Accidents happen and life goes on. But more recently Anne Bernays has decided, so to speak, to dig things up. She is a writer and that is any writer's job, or can be. The problem is that she doesn't know much about the accident itself (there wasn't, for example, any "gravel" to drive into), and I would guess that about motorcycles and the people who ride them she knows little beyond ordinary bias, which has it that anyone on a bike must be stupid or self-destructive. Bernays nevertheless makes harsh charges against Gardner, defining his death in a way that judges his life most unkindly. And she needs the motorcycle to help her. She has, she says, "natural skepticism about anyone who tempts fate by tooling around on a motorcycle." We know what she means, the way seventy percent of bike accidents are caused by people in cars who don't see what they hit. But there is also a touch of put-down here, and it doesn't work. Gardner was not tooling around. He was on his way to SUNY Binghamton to meet his students. He was going about a business he loved in a way he loved, and when he crashed his letters lay around him on the road. For Bernays, apparently, a man on a motorcycle is by definition a fool seeking ruin. If Gardner had been hit by lightning or a bad heart, there would have been shock and lament in response, but no raised eyebrows, no one saying I told you so. He died on a motorcycle, though, and instantly theories zoom out like bees exploding from a thicket.

Because it was an accident, lots of people feel sure that it wasn't. Gardner must have been drunk, which he was not, or racing like a bat out of hell, which he was not, but stuff like that keeps circulating nonetheless. The article by Bernays is hardly special in this regard. She has, however, put herself forward as a witness to what happened, and endorsed what she says with myths both high (art) and low (motorcycles). She says in *Boston*, the December '82 issue, that when she heard of Gardner's death she knew right away it might not be an accident, but more probably a case of "subintentional" suicide. She gives reasons for this conclusion, the Harley first of all, but also a glimpse of Gardner she got some weeks earlier at Bread Loaf Writers' Conference, an impression which convinced her that this man had lost his talent and his grip and was heading for disaster. Thus: "Gardner acted as if something awful were happening to him and he knew it and couldn't do anything to stop it." That is pretty grim. On the other hand, there's no doubt that behavior at Bread Loaf, almost everyone's, tends to be peculiar, though not necessarily in a negative way, and I'll remark more on that later. The point now is this: if Bernays starts with the mad biker myth and connects it with the myth of the mad artist – she calls Gardner "the writer as tamed wild man" – room for kindness and doubt isn't going to exist. As she says, Gardner *drove* his Harley off the road. *He* overturned *it*, a prodigious feat for 700 pounds of machine. But that, as some people think, is what bikers do.

LIKE HIS FATHER before him, who drove Harleys until he was seventy, Gardner traveled by motorcycle much of the time for more than thirty years. His accident, then, can't be kept apart from personal history and preference. I must also say that Gardner's behavior could be hectic and tormented on occasion, at least at Bread Loaf, which is the only place I knew him. Then too, anyone reading his fiction will see, in addition to fascination with monsters and grotesques, a darker strain in which, at the level of symbolic action and sometimes in theme, the desire for redemption and forgiveness seems caught up by some doom-laden spectral presence hard to define but definitely a part of Gardner's imagined world. None of this, however, yields specific conclusions. Half the important fiction of our time fits that description. Plenty of writers appear more than a little hectic and tormented, at least now and then. And Gardner, I must add immediately, was often tender, sanely as opposed to demonically brilliant, sometimes positively buddha-like. I saw him that way at Bread Loaf last summer.

If a pattern exists it isn't iron-clad or even complete. And accidents happen – unexpected, unforeseeable, not at all a matter of intention or will. Unless we abandon practical sense for some cheap or grand determinism, we must allow chance its terrifying role in our lives. I liked Gardner, I was shocked by his death, and gradually the question of specific circumstances (which I've looked into) has led me to consider what an accident is in itself, how it relates to the rest of a life, and how, when things like this happen, we rush faster than usual to judgment.

Unlike ordinary events, which we assess by their causes *and* their consequences, accidents are one-sided; we see them only from the back, blocked by an unaccountable gap keeping past and future discontinuous, the difference, perhaps, between normal evolution and sudden mutation. Between events in the usual sense and accidents there may be more similarity than we typically allow; but in the case of accidents we are more than normally alert to something in the occasion which is indeterminate, uncanny, undecidable, and for this reason accidents invite interpretation more readily than ordinary events. Because we don't know, we cover surprise by talking as if we did. There is, in an accident like Gardner's, an emptiness potent with meaning, or so we feel, and then to read it symbolically becomes a real temptation. Here in particular, anyone writing a life of Gardner will have to be on guard, and it occurs to me that professional biographers must have an infernal job, damned if they make sense of a life (fiction) and damned if they don't (mere massing of fact). In the construction of a biographical design, in search of a life's deeper logic, what will an accident look like? Not, perhaps, accidental.

The mistake would be to think of interpretation as something apart from the accident itself, as if one or another theory might win out as the event's true meaning, when at every moment the enormous element of undecidability leads us to see that any interpretation is part of something larger, a process of understanding that stays anchored in the odd obscurity of the accident itself. The FACTS are always there to start with, but these are at once too many and too few, contrary and incomplete, leading to imponderables enforced by the facts themselves. At this point MYTHS take over, cultural archetypes as well as local stories, all of them rooted in some actual detail or circumstance, but none able to dispose of the others or to cap the increasing flow of uncertainty. The feeling of the inadequacy of knowledge becomes more insistent and first appears as BLANKNESS, a senseless glare without depth or substance. This is part of the accident also, the mindlessness of it, as if facts, myths, the event itself were draining away. But then it doesn't drain away; the accident emerges from its preceding clutter, more real than before, something concrete and undeniable, partly open and partly withheld; and everything we know about it emphasizes what we don't know. At this stage, we are forced to admit that in the accident there is a genuine element of MYSTERY, not mere muddle or temporary lack of information, but something intrinsic to what an accident is. That, at least, has been the order of my own attempt to understand Gardner's wreck. First facts, then myths, then blankness, and finally mystery encompassing the lot.

The curve itself, for example. It's not what my son, who knows motorcycles, would call wicked bad, not anywhere near a right-angle turn, although it does swing to the left, which is to say it's not an inside curve and in the event of trouble a bike could be on the outside edge very fast. It's also blind for about 20 yards, it's not banked, it dips gently downward, and these are conditions less favorable to control than their opposites. Even so, coming into the turn at 50 or 55, braking lightly as a rider might decide, there simply should be no difficulty. And immediately, the curve opens into flat, straight highway ahead. Leaning into it, accelerating out, this curve should not have been trouble. Nor is there any gravel to cause a slide; the shoulder here is gritty dirt, level with the pavement, four to six feet of space between guardrail and road. Nothing, absolutely nothing at sane speeds to signal danger. This, in fact, is what perplexes me: there's nothing there. The strangeness of the accident is partly in the scene itself; no passerby would guess that this is where Gardner died. And he, of course, knew this road like the back of his hand; he'd biked to work this way many times. The other strange thing is that, from the diagram attached to the police report, it's clear that whatever occurred in the curve, the desperate part of the accident unfolded well past the pitch of the turn. What happened happened on the straightaway.

Perhaps defenders of the suicide theory will take comfort from my view of the accident's scene. But *look* at it. This just is not the place to kill yourself. The chances are fine for mutilation, which can happen as well in a supermarket parking lot, but to count on a fatal crash on this particular length of roadway would be very stupid indeed. Take the curve at 90, shoot off the highway and through the guardrail – even then you'd never make it down to the river. A tree, of course, anything solid would be enough to be lethal, and that, really, is the only clear option – some high-speed plunge off the road, not, as seems to have happened, some sort of drift onto the shoulder. Even at the subintentional level, as Bernays calls it, picking a place to die would seem to rule out this one. I regret talking like this, but failure to imagine the situation allows irresponsible theories their appeal. I guess I should also add that the countryside around Susquehanna offers all sorts of sharp turns and sheer drops, miles of tree-lined pavement and roadway-edging streams. No doubt someone desperate to die will grab any chance that offers itself, but anyone on a motorcycle will see excellent chances mile after mile. This place, by comparison, seems almost benign.

Unless, of course, something was in the road. Truckers usually know what they are doing, but any motorcyclist will tell you that people in cars are a hazard. They are talking, daydreaming, gawking at some signboard or oddity off to the side; they don't watch the road, they don't see motorcycles, and when they do they are often hostile. Coming up from the rear or approaching ahead, cars are always dangerous. But so far as we know (a woman living nearby was fairly sure), Gardner went into the curve alone. Another vehicle in the turn might well push a bike toward the shoulder; but that wasn't it. What about an animal? Small ones don't matter, a woodchuck or rabbit, but deer surely do. If one or more were in the road, or if one leapt from the bush into the path of the bike, disaster could indeed occur. My only objection is that the countryside along this stretch of road doesn't look like the kind of place deer generally use for a crossing; too much human habitation, no fields, the drop to the river too steep for easy access. But a deer there could have been. The nature of an accident is that something not normal, not expected, intervenes. And if it was a deer, or, say, a stray dog, we would never know. The other possibility is the kind of dog that attacks and gives chase, and here the local stories start. Twenty yards or so beyond the curve sits a trailer to the left of the highway. Four people I talked with told me that a big dog lives there, that the dog likes to chase motorcycles, that probably it was the dog that caused the accident. But no one had actually seen the dog. I looked for it, but couldn't find it either.

The accident, therefore, might have a very simple explanation, some small freak danger that, coming around the curve,

Gardner would have been upon almost instantly. The point is
that we don't know and can't find out. So in addition to the
bizarre behavior of the motorcycle after it came out of the
curve, there is also the possibility that something was in the
road and then gone. This is what I mean by undecidability. Although we must admit that absolutely anything might have
happened, our ignorance of what did happen is almost equally
absolute. The facts as we know them are just sufficient to spark
speculation, and when an accident is fatal, like this one, speculation – by which I mean mythmaking – can be wild and even
sinister.

Much of the information we have about the accident comes
from a woman (housewife, age 39, the police report says) who
was at home that afternoon, her house just above (i.e., going
into) the curve, and the windows were open. She knew Gardner
and, as often before, she heard him go by. From the sound of
the bike, she thinks he wasn't going especially fast. She also
thinks no other vehicle passed either way just before or after
the accident. What got her attention, first of all, was the sound
of a crash in the distance. According to the police report, what
happened next was this:

> I ran outside, down my driveway and down the road to where
> I could see an object lying on the roadway. I thought that a
> truck which was coming towards me had dropped something
> on the road. I first seen the truck down by the object on the
> road. The older model green flatbed truck pulling a small
> trailer, stopped where I was standing and the driver asked if
> I had called an ambulance because there was a man lying on
> the road.

She called an ambulance and when she returned to the road
the truck was gone. As the woman says, "I couldn't understand
why the driver of the truck didn't stay by the injured man." Nor
can we. I can imagine real brutality on the part of the driver,
but I cannot see that he had any part in the accident. The police
don't think so either. We will never know, but most likely the

truck had been traveling south, as it was when the woman first saw it, which means that its driver either saw the accident or came upon it directly afterward, then came onto the woman and asked her if she'd called an ambulance (didn't say she ought to), then left, reasons unknown. Although it must have been a farm truck, and could not have come from too far away, nobody in the area recognized it by its description. And needless to say, it hasn't been seen since.

Those are the facts, such as they are. Now the myth. The flat-bed truck almost immediately became, in everyone's reference to it, "the pickup truck" or simply "the pickup." And speculation has been endless. What was it doing out there? Why did it flee the scene of the accident? We see where this is going, yet it might not have assumed the authority it did had the woman not inadvertently contributed the key element: she said, or people say that she said, that her first impression was that the truck turned around. If that were so, then we have the "easy-rider" myth fullfledged. The bike and its rider were run off the road by the pickup, which then turned back to vanish as it came, out of nowhere. We remember the pickup truck at the end of the film *Easy Rider*, which after shotgunning one bike off the road, turns around to come back and blow away the second bike. That was, and I guess still is, a powerful image of American paranoia; it's also art waiting for life to follow suit. And it dovetails neatly with the myth of the mad biker and the "wild man" image of Gardner.

The fact that the truck disappeared, that we know *nothing* about it, will never cease to be a sticking point. But of course, the truck did not turn around. The woman's impression, while the situation was at a distance and unclear, was that *if* the object in the road had been dropped by the truck, *then* the truck must have come back for it. This initial impression was corrected immediately, but the woman mentioned that for a moment that's what she'd thought. From that simple slip the rumor spread, never mind that an old truck pulling a trailer could never take any curve fast enough to cause trouble. The truck played no part in the accident, but it did play a role in the way the accident came to be perceived. The driver of the truck was the first person on the scene; his behavior was sinister, and his disappearance leaves a real gap in our sense of what happened. In her article Anne Bernays does not mention the truck, and perhaps she never heard about it. Yet to call the article "Uneasy Writer" seems an unnecessary slam, and whether Bernays or an editor selected the title, it judges Gardner and hurts his loved ones.

Myths like the one about the pickup truck take their rise in circumstance; their seed is actual, but then they go on to account for everything and in the process fall apart. Their truth value ends up zero. The problem is that the hard facts, as we know them, also end up zero. I try to imagine what happened on that reach of roadway and I cannot. I especially cannot see how the machine could have hit its rider with such concentrated force if both rider and bike were still moving together. The sheer mechanics of it, they don't add up.

I remember talking with one of Gardner's Susquehanna friends, a young man about thirty who knows motorcycles, has a Harley of his own, and more than once had accompanied Gardner on trips. After the accident he'd gone out to the place and looked for tire markings. There were *some*, and from their confused pattern they seemed to reveal an intelligent struggle to get the motorcycle back on course safely. You could see, he told me, that Gardner had been fighting it. We were quiet for a few minutes, and then the young man, who clearly cares about Gardner, sighed and said, But you know, the marks were very faint, they could have been from something else, some other time or vehicle, and it's all, you see, not really readable.

LAST SUMMER Anne Bernays spent a few days at Bread Loaf and saw enough of Gardner to convince her that his soul was in terminal pain. The evening she found him "almost alone" and looking "very sad" she did not, evidently, go up to him; but there would have been much else happening, and lots of writers to meet, and it's easy to be swept along by the pleasures of the place. The conference can be like a three-ring circus, several main attractions at once. At least that's how it seemed to me the four summers I was there when Gardner was. The great enjoyment of it, in addition to the readings and the workshops and the non-stop excitement of so much excellent talk, is the communal atmosphere and the devotion with which men and women of proven talent pass on their craft and spirit to talented beginners. I have seen Gardner work very hard at this. Afternoons, when staff people would take a hike up the mountain, or run a Middlebury errand, or just sit somewhere in the shade with friends, Gardner would station himself in the big barn, the central meeting place, and be available to anyone who wanted his help. This was, I think, a point of honor with him, and Bernays concedes that as a teacher – an almost natural force moving young writers to realize their gifts – Gardner was extremely good.

I've seen Gardner steady as noon sun, giving himself with tribal care to any person with the guts or smarts to seek him out, and many did; sometimes it would look like a raid. I have also seen him join the rest of us at 5:30 for cocktails on the lawn or, if it rained, in the barn. And then go on after the evening reading and drink deep into the night. How much alcohol gets consumed at Bread Loaf is an astronomer's guess, and it's not that Gardner drank more than most, but that with him it was an *anabasis*, a march into the next day's dawn, and mainly for this reason: he loved, sought out, maybe really needed, community of talk. Not every night, but enough, he'd engage in discussion, excitement would spread like a message from the capitol, and a small knot of writers, equal in thought, equal in drink, would gather to fathom Gardner and themselves. Literature, politics, God, no subject smaller would do, and off things would go, Gardner as orator, sophist, inquisitor by turns, talking on and on, elated with ideas and the sport of it, playful, earnest, sometimes as if possessed – and all the time he, like the others around him, would be sipping away, in Gardner's case mainly gin, not noticing how much or how fast it went down. This sort of event wasn't unusual among members of the conference, but Gardner was different in that he'd seldom just stop. The lateness of the hour seemed to mean nothing to him, perhaps because in his other life, as a working writer, his habit was to start writing at midnight and keep on until five or six in the morning. As long as there could be talk, those Bread Loaf nights, there would be, and much of it was very fine. It could also lead to drunken nonsense, of course, but at his best Gardner could be a little like Socrates at the Symposium, talking real philosophy, drinking everyone else under the table. And I can see that if, late next morning, Bernays happened to pass Gardner on his way to the barn for some coffee, she might well get the impression that "something awful" was happening to him because it was – a hangover out of this world, the world itself only starting to return.

Making her case for accident-as-suicide, Bernays offers an outright list of things she thinks contributed to Gardner's subintentional death-wish. In truly desperate cases I suppose that any additional small burden, or an aggregate assuming a sort of critical mass, might drive a person past saving. But even at that, some of Bernays's observations seem odd. It's true, as she points out, that Gardner got "dumped on" for writing *On Moral Fiction* and that his last novel, *Mickelsson's Ghosts*, was received with mainly negative reviews. But that's the lot of writers, and the real question about Gardner was whether he intended, like any novelist, to push on. Bernays also reminds us that Gardner "had had cancer," but goodness, any person saved from cancer might be extra glad to be alive. Bernays goes on to point out that Gardner had "been married and divorced twice" and was about to be married again; yet what this reveals, beyond remarkable faith in life, is hard to see. Is any of this, or all of it together, reason for suicide? Bernays thinks so. Her deeper logic is that in every way – literary, personal, biological – Gardner was failing.

Bernays mentions two occasions at Bread Loaf when, in her

view, Gardner's performance certified his failure as a writer. One was his reading of his story "Cæsar and the Werewolf" to an evening audience. The story was fascinating in idea but pedestrian in style, and also a species of medieval fable-making that Gardner, but not many of the rest of us, liked. To Bernays the story seemed disjointed and overlong, and her mind, she says, wandered. And then it came to her: "What is this monster doing in the core of a straight narrative?" That's offered as a criticism of the story, although it *could* be taken as an intelligent insight into the general structure of Gardner's fiction. Everywhere, in Gardner's novels, monsters and monstrous texts preside at the heart of straight narratives. What this tells us of Gardner might be worth pursuing, but Bernays doesn't see it. Nor does she seem to know that at Bread Loaf the audience regularly sat through this kind of reading when Gardner's turn came. Summer before last he read an openly mindless tale about a female detective disguised in a cheap-laughs beard. Before that it was funny-flat stuff from a child's bestiary. Why Gardner insisted on this kind of reading I don't know. Perhaps he refused to be in competition with his peers, Stanley Elkin and John Irving among them. Perhaps, as in *October Light,* he wanted to see if a sophisticated audience, like the old woman trapped with her smugglers' tale, would find "trash" to its liking. Hard to say, but the reading was standard for Gardner; perverse, but not a signal of defeat. And after the reading I very much doubt that, as Bernays thinks, he "must have realized he'd blown it."

One last item, more interesting than Bernays suggests. Staff people at Bread Loaf give a talk or lecture, usually about craft, and when Gardner gave his he provoked, as Bernays reports, bafflement and anger, at least in some quarters. He started ten minutes late and then only talked for about fifteen minutes, although it wasn't at night, nor did he walk off any stage, as Bernays describes the event. But she wasn't there and has had to rely on secondary sources. He did begin by saying that he was "not interested in literature any more," a statement which

Bernays takes as a declaration of Gardner's capitulation as a writer. But that's not the end of it, nor did Gardner ramble on about "political injustice" without point or design. His first remark was meant to shock, which it did, and so did the rest of his remarks, mainly about political awareness as a writing tool, a theme indeed disturbing to writers in the current genteel tradition, as afraid of politics in art as the Victorians were of sex. "You are not writing importantly," Gardner went on to say, "if you're not writing politically." He wasn't endorsing propaganda or programmatic writing; he meant, as one might see, that the overwhelming and possibly fatal dimension of modern experience is political, from our terror of nuclear threat to our deeply personal shame for what our government sometimes does in our name, and if literature doesn't touch this part of our lives it will surely lose its claim to importance. Like many of us, Gardner was alarmed by the way politics disrupts the soul; and for a novelist to be concerned with responsibility and consequence isn't so strange. Gardner also said that "to write greatly you must feel greatly," a judgment that must have sunk many a cloistered heart then and there.

If Gardner's lecture caused a feeling of distress to hang over the conference "like a radioactive cloud," as Bernays reconstructs it, her metaphor is especially insensitive, considering Gardner's urgent message. It also hints that Bread Loaf is exactly the place to go to get away from it all, just *belles lettres*, some cocktail conversation, and more *belles lettres*. But that's not the case. If talk of politics in relation to literature upset some people, others of us, that particular summer, had been talking of little else since the start of the conference. The Bread Loaf session of 1982 was different from earlier meetings because, for the first time openly and with a good deal of passion, the idea began to circulate that art can no longer be held separate from the kind of political torment maiming our age and spirit. Some confrontation there will have to be, darker energies distilled, a harder vision of being in the world. So Gardner's lecture did not come out of nowhere. It might have signaled a change in his thinking about literature, but it broadcast no admission of defeat.

The portrait of Gardner that Bernays sketches for us doesn't hold up – not the mad biker, not the writer as wild man, not the failed genius. Concerning Gardner's accident, she is innocent of the facts and blind to the mystery, and she makes her case for suicide in terms of an inner logic such as only myths possess. Of the three accounts of the accident – the newspaper report, the police report, the literary report – only Bernays's makes sense all the way. She is that far removed.

THE LAST TIME I saw Gardner was departure time, Sunday morning, the end of the 1982 session at Bread Loaf. My son and I were loading our bike onto its trailer and Gardner came over to give us a hand. Then we said goodbye and he was gone. Speaking of his work the year before, he'd said: "When you look back there's lots of bales in the field, but ahead it's all still to mow." The rural metaphor was typical of him; so was the ambition, the natural look forward. The day of the accident, Gardner was planning to meet students in Binghamton, and later that afternoon he was coming back to cast the musical – *Marvin's on the Distant Shore* – that he had written for, and with, his friends at the Laurel Street Theatre in Susquehanna. It was a communal affair, and more people wanted to be in it than there were parts, so Gardner intended to spend the evening writing new roles. This was art for everyone, Gardner had done it before, and the town loved it. So, it appears, did Gardner. He was getting married in less than a week, and years of work on a translation of *Gilgamesh* had just been finished. Soon *On Becoming a Novelist* would appear, and his close friends tell me that Gardner was full of plans of *all* sorts, just like the old days.

And yet, all of us lead more than one life, artists especially. The mind moves at different levels, the spirit is always warring with itself, not content with external terrors only. No one of us is privy to the whole soul's show, not our own, not another's,

which is what makes art so valuable and easy usage of a word
like "subintentional" suspect. We also know, since it's how we
live, that ebb and flow is constant, that decline and renewal is
life's first pattern. This is true for artists in particular, who more
than the rest of us use their work to live by, charting and steering, coming home and setting forth repeatedly. And even when
it comes to the worst, as survivors of all kinds remind us, the
fact that a man is down is no sign he's out.

That said, I must now say the rest. Two of Gardner's dearest
friends told me that within a month of the accident he had said,
straight out, that he felt like he was going to die. One friend
feels he said it with a touch of fear, the other thinks his mood
was brave and accepting. Neither, at the time, got the idea that
Gardner meant suicide. What exactly he did mean isn't obvious;
he didn't know, and neither do we. A man turning fifty might
indeed sense a sea-change upon him. To feel in the presence
of death is not uncommon when fundamental transformation
begins. And there will be an end – some part of the self sloughed
off, past solutions to life and art abandoned to open a future.
None of this calls for an accident. We have to be careful in such
judgments; the blankness of the accident becomes a blindness
in the judging mind, stupid for design and retribution.

There is no life without its mystery, and sorting out the mystery, which is what biographers do, will have to accommodate
not only facts and myths and regions of blankness, but also, in
the case of a writer's life, the mystery of his works. I cannot do
that here, of course, but two examples will be enough to suggest
how difficult and fearful such a task might be. "Redemption"
is one of Gardner's late stories, published in a collection in 1981,
and it opens this way:

> One day in April – a clear, blue day when there were crocuses
> in bloom – Jack Hawthorne ran over and killed his brother,
> David.

The accident is then described, faithful point by point to that other accident in Gardner's life, when as a boy of twelve he was operating the farm machine under which his younger brother fell and died. The next paragraph speaks not of Jack's grief but of the father's, and in the third paragraph, still with the father, we get this:

> ...he would ride away on his huge, darkly thundering Harley-Davidson 80, trying to forget, morbidly dwelling on what he'd meant to put behind him...or...for the hundredth time, about suicide, hunting in mixed fear and anger for some reason not to miss the next turn, fly off to the right of the next iron bridge onto the moonlit gray rocks and black water below.

A psychoanalyst would grab at such a passage, pointing to the father's role as super-ego and enforcer of guilt, suggesting in the dream of suicide the means of redemption. For the young man in Gardner's story, however, the burden of the accident is lifted through music and the dæmon-empowered world of art. He takes up study of the French horn and finds, as his mentor, a figure greatly more powerful than the figure of the father, and it is this stronger spirit's blessing the young man receives. Few of us believe any more that through art our sins shall be forgiven us; but perhaps it's not too much to think that through art a state of provisional grace can be gained, a kind of redemption renewed daily in the practice of one's craft. When Gardner was coming into his stride as an artist and a teacher, his favorite remark to his students was that "art saves souls." I guess we know what that means, in a grand vague way, but in retrospect it points to a darker, more personal vision and might be taken as Gardner's comment on his own career. That he was possessed and driven he readily admitted, and in *On Becoming a Novelist* he put it this way:

> Dæmonic compulsiveness can kill as easily as it can save. The true novelist must be at once driven and indifferent....Drivenness only helps if it forces the writer not to suicide but to the

making of splendid works of art, allowing him indifference to whether or not the novel sells, whether or not it's appreciated. Drivenness is trouble for both the novelist and his friends; but no novelist, I think, can succeed without it.

OBVIOUSLY GARDNER believed that art should help us live our lives, the better to enjoy, the better to endure; and it seems clear that he also expected writing to help the writer – art, that is, as *good works*. And now, because of the accident, we ask if Gardner's faith had failed him. But because of the accident, we can't know. Like any accident, this one does as much to break the design as to complete it. And because of it, nothing in Gardner's life is decidable finally. People say he was going through hard changes. People say he was on the mend. Rebirth, too, has its harrowing hours. And what if he wasn't healing, or not yet? What, even supposing enormous pain, does it tell us that on a pleasant afternoon he decided to travel by motorcycle? A man can feel utterly awful and then go out into the crystal day, move through realms of changing light across the road, feel the power of the machine bearing him kindly, surely, and be at home in the homeless wind, the burden abruptly lifted. He can have terrible visions and at moments like this feel beyond them and blessed. I describe it that way because that's the way we spoke of it at Bread Loaf. There are times, we agreed, when a motorcycle clears the mind.

Much of what I've said can be turned around and be made to go the other way. I take the risk because Gardner's death can't be used to measure his life, not soundly or in fairness, and where there's doubt there ought to be kindness. The way Gardner died does not clear or confirm, but rather opens and questions any settled version of his life. Having got this far, moreover, I don't see much choice but to open matters further, and perhaps at this point a poetic image will work best. I quote a passage from the last pages of *Grendel*, exactly as Gardner quotes it himself in *On Becoming a Novelist*, for what it says about accidents, and then, in Gardner's own commentary, for what he says about himself. This is Gardner's monster dying after a fatal wound:

> No one follows me now. I stumble again and with my one weak arm I cling to the huge twisted roots of an oak. I look down past stars to a terrifying darkness. I seem to recognize the place, but it's impossible. "Accident," I whisper. I will fall. I seem to desire the fall, and though I fight it with all my will I know in advance that I can't win. Standing baffled, quaking with fear, three feet from the edge of a nightmare cliff, I find myself, incredibly, moving toward it. I look down, down into bottomless blackness, feeling the dark power moving in me like an ocean current, some monster inside me, deep sea wonder, dread night monarch astir in his cave, moving me slowly to my voluntary tumble into death.

I suppose the allegorical force of this scene, in retrospect, leaps at us like the findings of a blood test. After the accident all manner of things take on meaning where none was before, a circumstance that calls for going slow. But let us see Gardner's commentary, keeping in mind that if at the moment of death there is a way in which necessity and chance become one, this is never seen, by Gardner or his monster, as the logic of suicide. Here is Gardner's reflection:

> "Accident!" – that is, Beowulf's victory has no moral meaning; all life is chance. But the fear that it may not all be accident strikes back instantly, prodded a little by childhood notions of the cross – blood, guilt, one's desperate wish to be a good boy, be loved by one's parents and by that terrifying superfather whose otherness cannot be more frighteningly expressed than by the fact that he lives beyond the stars. So for all his conscious belief that it's all accident, Grendel *chooses* death, morally aligning himself with God (hence trying to save himself); that is, against his will he notices he seems to "desire the fall."

The world envisioned here, and the imagination at work to see it, are as far removed from modern psychology as Gardner's novel is from literary realism. The vision here is religious, very nearly medieval, and then not full revelation but only a trace, since it's only in the moment of the monster's choice that the vision exists. That's as much, I think, as Gardner felt he could hope for. But it's there, and while it lasts chance plays no part. Events are informed by the mystery of divine intent, accidents in particular, because they cannot be accounted for or fully explained. They come out of the blue, summoned by God's will. And that is how Gardner's monster, appalled by death's nothingness, eager to feel its necessity, comes to see his fall. The scene doesn't represent a suicide; it enacts the agony of the monstrous soul coming to terms with its death, and it ought to go without saying that any soul, to itself, appears monstrous. Grendel's choice isn't to live *or* die, being fatally wounded already. His choice is to accept the death that is upon him and in this moment — which must, after all, feel ultimate — to divine a power greater than himself. Dante's comment in the *Paradiso* was In His will is our peace. The street version is that when your number's up it's up.

Gardner's religious view is valid. But no latter-day reader, having looked closely at the death scene in *Grendel* and then at Gardner's commentary, will be satisfied to let things rest in God's hands. This is perhaps our problem, but the Freudian content can't be denied. The idea of accident, we would say, is overdetermined; it includes childhood notions of guilt and the cross, a boy's desperate wish to be good and be loved, choice as part of dying and death itself as redemption. In view of Gardner's accident these nodes of meaning seem to lock into design, perhaps the structure of Grendel's fate most of all — first a wound got by chance, and then the desire for a voluntary fall that feels compelled. How much weight can stuff of this kind bear? We are again in the realm of uncertainty, but to take it all the way is easy, and we shall end up with just the sort of symmetry most pleasing to our taste, exquisite in its precision, terrible in what it presumes to reveal. Between Gardner's first accident and his last, the life and work of an exceedingly gifted man becomes the long dying of a monster fatally wounded, seeking to fall.

So yes, we can go to that length, all the way and perhaps all the more boldly for Gardner's comment that when he wrote the scene of Grendel dying, he was in a "trance-like state." But if we pull back even a little, it's apparent that something trance-like happens to us as well, the compulsion of metaphor collapsing restraint, urging us onward to sum things up. The coherent design, as I've outlined it, rests on two short bits of texts out of thousands of pages in many books; evidence of this kind would never stand except, of course, in an essay with literary leanings or a case history with clinical intent. We see, too, how we must isolate such passages to make them assume the sought-for significance. And then there remains the actual place on the highway; to go there and attempt to feel the authority of the design is to discover that in saying what happened we seem to believe that to think is to be. And there is still the accident itself, the hole in all our thinking, the piece of the puzzle that rolled off the asphalt into the grass.

Set on by darkness, imagination can go any length, even this: the man who rode the monster in himself, allowing its power to infuse and carry his art, was the man who rode the Harley all his life, staying with the risk and keeping it under good enough control, determined that this monster of a machine, like the demon in his soul, would get him to wherever he might need or be required to go. But its power wasn't finally his, neither the horror in the heart nor the big bike he trusted enough not to fear. He saw no accident coming, but in actual fact the motorcycle hit him hard enough to kill him. The most shocking thing about the accident, at least as the police wrote it up, is that at no point did bike or rider collide with *anything*. Except, of course, each other. Living some hundred yards around the curve, the woman by her window heard the crash. What crash? The only possible moment of impact was the instant when, after moving along the corridor of the shoulder, the motorcycle hit the pavement midway in its long careen.

Maybe it bounced, maybe went end over end, but it didn't just skid and drag, it turned on its rider with vast force, then was up and went on.

That way of seeing it makes sense to me, as I think it might to others who know motorcycles. In the end, though, it's only one more story—another metaphor ordaining design. And taken to its extravagant limit, it shows the craziness that comes from fighting the void. The sober fact is that what happened that September afternoon is never going to be known. Whatever we think, it will be theory washed in myth. We might understand what we can, and then let it be. Gardner has his death, his dignity, his uniqueness as strange and unyielding as the "accident that took his life." That's how the *Sun-Bulletin* put it. And in some way really, that's what it was, a life that an accident took.

PHILLIP MOFFITT

The Power
of One Woman

IN MY HEART, the Christmas season will always belong to a long-deceased southern Appalachian mountain woman whose name was Etta Lee.

She was one of a special breed of women who once inhabited the hills and valleys of Kentucky, Tennessee, Virginia, and North Carolina.

How can one describe to an outsider the beauty, the agony, the mystery of these women?

They were the daughters of dirt farmers, laborers, and coal miners whose ancestors had come to America's shores poor and uneducated and had headed west in search of economic opportunity but never made it past the Appalachians.

Being born in those mountains and growing up poor in those little communities meant embracing a particular way of life – a life of doing for yourself, caring for your own, and suffering silently. The Appalachian women, as Etta Lee used to tell me, "took their strength from the mountains and from living day to day." It was a way of life that created women with tough, worn bodies, fixed, guarded faces, and eyes that had learned the danger in expecting too much from the world.

The specter of defeat, the humiliation of "not having anything decent," of not being able to provide properly for the children, was the hardest cross these Appalachian women had to bear. It was not just their own failed hopes with which they had to contend, but also the fears and defeat of both their own fathers and the men they'd married. Those proud, solitary mountain men harbored a rage born of the frustration of knowing they had no promise in life and nowhere to go. That sort of rage finds expression in easily injured pride, and its companions are physical violence and emotional brutality. The Appalachian women, as daughters and wives, often suffered the blows, the hard words, the stony silences of that rage and had to live their lives weighted by its unrelenting tension.

It is no wonder that these women turned inward, considering life's mysteries in terms of the moods of the mountain weather, the wild flowers and trees of the woods, and the tales they told their children of heroes and villains and ghosts and miracles. They prepared their children not to surmount great heights, but to endure and to suffer the lot that God had given them.

In the 1930s and 1940s the outside world started to touch the Appalachians. The government built decent roads and dammed the rivers, and industry began to move in. Suddenly the men had new prospects, the women a better standard of living. The level of education rose dramatically, and the isolation of these communities gradually ended. As their communities joined the mainstream of American life these Appalachian women started to disappear. Today, in the mountain towns, one will occasionally come across a woman who stands out from the crowd, and one can easily guess her ancestry by her earthiness, that strength that characterized the southern Appalachian women and defined Etta Lee.

Etta Lee was special even among this special breed. She was born in Damascus, Virginia, in 1892, to the Dickenson family, whose ancestry was probably a mixture of European blood and maybe a little American Indian. Looking for better work anywhere, the family moved to Tennessee. At age fourteen Etta Lee married a strapping young man, a sharecropper's son named Della Wayland Moffitt, who had nothing but a strong back to recommend him. Both Etta Lee and Della had had only about a second-grade education. Theirs was a hard marriage and a hard life. Della got a job working for the Carolina, Clinchfield, and Ohio Railway laying ties as the line extended from Tennessee to the Carolinas. For the first three years of their marriage Etta and Della lived in the confines of a single railway freight car. As the railway would extend another mile, a little engine called a dinkey would pull along all the cars housing the work crew. It was a world of backbreaking work, uncaring bosses, and meanspirited men; fights were as popular as the weekly payday. Della learned to set concrete block, lay brick, measure lumber with his naked eye, and having acquired these skills, he was finally able to settle down in the 1920s, to work in a cement factory. Etta bore four children, had two or three miscarriages, and endured. Della was strong, hard, quick-tempered, and domineering, but Etta was a fighter and held her own – she once knocked him unconscious with an iron skillet. Theirs was a union not of similar sensibilities but of singular wills, with each standing steadfast behind a barrier of watchful strength.

In my earliest memories of her, Etta Lee stands about five foot five, with brown eyes and black hair. By that time she was in her fifties. She was small-boned, weighing no more than about a hundred pounds, and always seemed somewhat fragile, but never timid or weak. In fact, in my memories she seems less a physical presence than an emotional one – a presence not visible to others, like the wind in those mountain valleys, rustling and touching but never seeming to have a place of origin.

She did not behave like a typical grandmother. There were no hugs and kisses or praise for my abilities or interest in my accomplishments, nor would I have thought to tell her my problems or seek her advice. Yet she was the most important person for me in those formative years, and the person with whom I spent the most time. In retrospect, I could describe her as having somehow been assigned to that little boy, to give him a kind of comfort, to train his mind and shape his emotions. But that description does not capture the actual experience of being a five-year-old, lying for hours on end underneath a tall pine tree on an old homemade quilt and listening to her soft, slightly raspy voice telling me stories of the mountains, of the railroad, of impoverished life. It does not capture being eight years old and eating graham crackers with peanut butter while sitting at an old, chipped kitchen table and listening to tales of mountain spooks and of unrequited love. Nor does it capture the transforming power of being nine or ten years old and being told the full story of one's own father as only a mother could know it, and the story of one's father's father as only a wife could tell it. They were real stories, without rose coloring; adult stories of human weakness, of betrayal, of domination – stories without heroes and happy endings, but also without self-pity or defeat. Life as it is.

Why did she tell me those stories? How often I've wondered about that. She was a storyteller with a real gift, and I was a born listener. She certainly never told such stories to her other grandchildren, but that doesn't mean I was her favorite; that honor belonged to a slightly older cousin. Was I a recipient of her legacy, the one chosen to bear witness to her having lived, loved, and suffered? Did she sense that I would use, even desperately *need*, the understanding of life's ways that her stories provided? Whatever the reason, she did it, and in doing so, she shaped my development as no one else could have.

She taught a young mind to assume that all behavior was shaped by a person's history and to seek out that history. She determined the emotional makeup of that child, such that he found comfort in knowing the truth, even if it was a horrible truth, and saw that no matter what his misery, he had no monopoly on pain nor any extra rights to happiness. She led that little boy to the understanding that there is a cause for everything.

How can a boy act out his rage when he knows the cause of it, knows that this father and his father's father before him suffered the same rage? How can the boy's view of his parents not be inevitably altered when each week he hears more of their story, is forced to see them in the context of *their* struggle for happiness? How can he not be affected by learning that his school principal had suffered a broken heart as a young woman and never recovered?

I was a quiet but intractably independent child who would easily bristle at all adult authority. Etta Lee never acted as that authority, choosing instead to be on my side without judgment. When I began smoking at age nine, she would buy me a pack of cigarettes each week. Is it any wonder that I stopped smoking at fourteen? When I needed simply to go somewhere, there was always a place in her house, and she would let me be, never asking questions. If I needed to pretend to be at her house while actually wandering the town, she gave her silent cooperation. She simply assumed that I was responsible for myself, and in so doing she helped me become so.

She had an extraordinary talent for seeing the true character of a person or place. I vividly recall our discussing my younger brothers and sister when they were still toddlers, and she told me the specific personalities they would develop as adults. And they did, just as she'd said. What in hindsight seems most astonishing, however, although I accepted it without question at the time, is that she could describe places she had never seen — she had never been to a zoo or a seaside beach, yet she knew about them, about their essence. I would go to these places years later and they would be as she'd said. She would tell me about living in a big city, how politics worked. And I now know how right she was. This woman who could barely read or write, who could never escape her long-suffering role in life, who never traveled more than a hundred miles from where she grew up, could project the experiences of her own limited life onto the world as a whole. She could make a leap of imagination that most people cannot.

At twelve I became much too involved in running around with a crowd of older teenagers in the neighborhood and with chasing after girls to have time for our relationship. Moreover, there were younger siblings who needed her more, and age and illness were changing her dramatically. So our intense time together ended. I entered my teenage years, a man-child whose combination of understanding and naiveté caused an increasing alienation from my peers – a fact I hid as best I could. Always I searched for those who saw the world as I did, and almost never could I find them. Teenagers, filled with their excessive adrenaline, are driven to explore the world outside themselves. Etta Lee, with her stories and dispassionate observations, had turned me too much inside myself to be an enthusiastic explorer of the world around me.

It has been twenty-five years since the days of our talks, and she has been dead fifteen of them. Over the years I have come to realize how deep and mysterious her knowledge was, and what a price she paid to acquire it day by day in those Appalachian mountains. I know now that I simply had the good fortune to be there at a certain time in her life, when she was past her personal struggle but not her vigorous vitality. She still had the energy to capture the reality and the drama of life, but she had no need to twist what she told me to satisfy her own emotional needs.

The little boy who listened to her gained an advantage. He learned to see through her eyes without having to pay the price she had paid in living. Although it took him years to realize it, she provided him with the power of possibility to escape his own rage and to overcome his own fear of failure.

But Etta Lee never found out how to use her talents to overcome the ache in her own heart. Probably it was in looking away from pain that she'd developed her abilities, and they came to fruition too late in her life to help her rise above her own circumstances. I do not know. Nor do I presume to judge this remarkable woman.

On a wet and cold and very lonely Christmas Eve some sixteen years ago I realized how similar my nature was to Etta Lee's. I realized that despite my outward drive for success and worldly accomplishment, I too was of those hills and valleys, and my days, like hers, could be filled with the sweet sadness of observing life from the isolation of dark mountains.

On New Year's Day that year, 1969, my resolution was that I would seek my peace in the world and let love and friendship warm the chill of life's disappointments. Believing that one can choose whether to be flooded by the sorrow or the joy of human existence, I vowed to escape those mountain shadows, to take that step Etta Lee could not take herself. Unfortunately, it is not so easy to leave behind that which is carried in the heart, and each Christmas Eve since then, in my annual hour of reckoning, I discover how much further I still must journey. But I do not give up, for I know that I will try once more in the name of Etta Lee.

BRENDA PETERSON

✖

Growing Up Game

When I went off to college my father gave me, as part of my tuition, 50 pounds of moose meat. In 1969, eating moose meat at the University of California was a contradiction in terms. Hippies didn't hunt. I lived in a rambling Victorian house which boasted sweeping circular staircases, built-in lofts, and a landlady who dreamed of opening her own health food restaurant. I told my housemates that my moose meat in its nondescript white butcher paper was from a side of beef my father had bought. The carnivores in the house helped me finish off such suppers as sweet and sour moose meatballs, mooseburgers (garnished with the obligatory avocado and sprouts), and mooseghetti. The same dinner guests who remarked upon the lean sweetness of the meat would have recoiled if I'd told them the not-so-simple truth: that I grew up on game, and the moose they were eating had been brought down, with one shot through his magnificent heart, by my father – a man who had hunted all his life and all of mine.

One of my earliest memories is of crawling across the vast continent of crinkled linoleum in our Forest Service cabin kitchen, down splintered back steps, through wildflowers growing wheat-high. I was eye-level with grasshoppers who scolded me on my first solo trip outside. I made it to the shed, a cool and comfortingly square shelter that held phantasmagoric metal parts; they smelled good, like dirt and grease. I had played a long time in this shed before some maternal shriek made me lift up on my haunches to listen to those urgent, possessive sounds that were my name. Rearing up, my head bumped into something hanging in the dark; gleaming white, it felt sleek and cold against my cheek. Its smell was dense and musty and not unlike the slabs of my grandmother's great arms after her cool, evening sponge baths. In that shed I looked up and saw the flensed body of a doe; it swung gently, slapping my face. I felt then as I do even now when eating game: horror and awe and hunger.

Growing up those first years on a forest station high in the Sierra was somewhat like belonging to a white tribe. The men hiked off every day into their forest and the women stayed behind in the circle of official cabins, breeding. So far away from a store, we ate venison and squirrel, rattlesnake and duck. My brother's first rattle, in fact, was from a King Rattler my father killed as we watched, by snatching it up with a stick and winding it, whiplike, around a redwood sapling. Rattlesnake tastes just like chicken, but has many fragile bones to slither one's way through; we also ate salmon, rabbit, and geese galore. The game was accompanied by such daily garden dainties as fried okra, mustard greens, corn fritters, wilted lettuce (our favorite because of that rare, blackened bacon), new potatoes and peas, stewed tomatoes, barbecued butter beans.

I was 4 before I ever had a beef hamburger and I remember being disappointed by its fatty, nothing taste and the way it fell apart at the seams whenever my teeth sank into it. Smoked pork shoulder came much later in the South; and I was 21, living in New York City, before I ever tasted leg of lamb. I approached that glazed rack of meat with a certain guilty self-consciousness, as if I unfairly stalked those sweet-tempered white creatures myself. But how would I explain my squeamishness to those urban sophisticates? How explain that I was shy with mutton when I had been bred on wild things?

Part of it, I suspect, had to do with the belief I'd also been bred on — we become the spirit and body of animals we eat. As a child eating venison I liked to think of myself as lean and lovely just like the deer. I would never be caught dead just grazing while some man who wasn't even a skillful hunter crept up and konked me over the head. If someone wanted to hunt me, he must be wily and outwitting. He must earn me.

My father had also taught us as children that animals were our brothers and sisters under their skin. They died so that we might live. And of this sacrifice we must be mindful. "God make us grateful for what we are about to receive," took on a new meaning when one knew the animal's struggle pitted against our own appetite. We also used *all* the animal so that an elk became elk steaks, stew, salami, and sausage. His head and horns went on the wall to watch us more earnestly than any babysitter, and every Christmas Eve we had a ceremony of making our own moccasins for the new year out of whatever Father had tanned. "Nothing wasted," my father would always say, or, as we munched on sausage cookies made from moosemeat or venison, "Think about who you're eating." We thought of ourselves as intricately linked to the food chain. We knew, for example, that a forest fire meant, at the end of the line, we'd suffer too. We'd have buck stew instead of venison steak and the meat would be stringy, withered-tasting because in the animal kingdom, as it seemed with humans, only the meanest and leanest and orneriest survived.

Once when I was in my early teens, I went along on a hunting trip as the "main cook and bottle-washer," though I don't remember any bottles; none of these hunters drank alcohol. There was something else coursing through their veins as they rose long before dawn and disappeared, returning to my little camp most often dragging a doe or pheasant or rabbit. We ate innumerable cornmeal-fried catfish, had rabbit stew seasoned only with blood and black pepper.

This hunting trip was the first time I remember eating game as a conscious act. My father and Buddy Earl shot a big doe and she lay with me in the back of the tarp-draped station wagon all the way home. It was not the smell I minded, it was the glazed great, dark eyes and the way that head flopped around crazily on what I knew was once a graceful neck. I found myself petting this doe, murmuring all those graces we'd been taught long ago as children. *Thank you for the sacrifice, thank you for letting us be like you so that we can grow up strong as game.* But there was an uneasiness in me that night as I bounced along in the back of the car with the deer.

What was uneasy is still uneasy – perhaps it always will be. It's not easy when one really starts thinking about all this: the eating game, the food chain, the sacrifice of one for the other. It's never easy when one begins to think about one's most basic actions, like eating. Like becoming what one eats: lean and lovely and mortal.

Why should it be that the purchase of meat at a butcher shop is somehow more righteous than eating something wild? Perhaps it has to do with our collective unconscious that sees the animal bred for slaughter as doomed. But that wild doe or moose might make it without the hunter. Perhaps on this primitive level of archetype and unconscious knowing we even believe that what's wild lives forever.

My father once told this story around a hunting campfire. His own father, who raised cattle during the Depression on a dirt farm in the Ozarks, once fell on such hard times that he had to butcher the pet lamb for supper. My father, bred on game or their own hogs all his life, took one look at the family pet on that meat platter and pushed his plate away from him. His siblings followed suit. To hear my grandfather tell it, it was the funniest thing he'd ever seen. "They just couldn't eat Bo-Peep," Grandfather said. And to hear my father tell it years later around that campfire, it was funny, but I saw for the first time his sadness. And I realized that eating had become a conscious act for him that day at the dinner table when Bo-Peep offered herself up.

Now when someone offers me game I will eat it with all the qualms and memories and reverence with which I grew up eating it. And I think it will always be this feeling of horror and awe and hunger. And something else – full knowledge of what I do, what I become.

BARRY LOPEZ

�֍

Story at Anaktuvuk Pass

ONE SUMMER EVENING in a remote village in the Brooks
Range of Alaska, I sat among a group of men listening to
hunting stories about the trapping and pursuit of animals. I
was particularly interested in several incidents involving wolverine, in part because a friend of mine was studying wolverine
in Canada, among the Cree, but, too, because I find this animal
such an intense creature. To hear about its life is to learn more
about fierceness.

Wolverine are not intentionally secretive, hiding their lives
from view, but they are seldom observed. The range of their
known behavior is less than that of, say, bears or wolves. Still,
that evening, no gratuitous details were set out. This was somewhat odd, for wolverine easily excite the imagination; they can
loom suddenly in the landscape with authority, with an aura
larger than their compact physical dimensions, drawing one's
immediate and complete attention. Wolverine also have a de-
served reputation for resoluteness in the worst of winters, for
ferocious strength. But neither did these attributes induce the
men to embellish.

I listened carefully to these stories, taking pleasure in the
sharply observed detail surrounding the dramatic thread of
events. The story I remember most vividly was about a man
hunting a wolverine from a snow machine in the spring. He

followed the animal's tracks for several miles over rolling tundra in a certain valley. Soon he caught sight ahead of a dark spot on the crest of a hill – the wolverine pausing to look back. The hunter was catching up, but each time he came over a rise the wolverine was looking back at him from the next rise, just out of range. The hunter topped one more rise and met the wolverine bounding toward him. Before he could pull his rifle from its scabbard the wolverine flew across the engine cowl and the windshield, hitting him square in the chest. The hunter scrambled his arms wildly trying to get the wolverine out of his lap and fell over as he did so. The wolverine jumped clear as the snow machine rolled over, and fixed the man with a stare. He had not bitten, not even scratched the man. Then the wolverine walked away. The man thought of reaching for the gun, but no, he did not.

The other stories were like this, not so much making a point as evoking something about contact with wild animals that would never be completely understood.

When the stories were over, four or five of us walked out of the home of our host. The surrounding land, in the persistent light of a far northern summer, was still visible for miles – the striated, pitched massifs of the Brooks Range; the shy, willow-lined banks of the John River flowing south from Anaktuvuk Pass; and the flat tundra plain, opening with great affirmation to the north. The landscape seemed alive because of the stories. It was precisely these ocherous tones, this kind of willow, exactly this austerity that had informed the wolverine narratives. I felt exhilaration, and a deeper confirmation of what I had heard. The mundane tasks that awaited me I anticipated now with pleasure. The stories had renewed in me a sense of the purpose of my life.

This feeling, an inexplicable renewal of enthusiasm after storytelling, is familiar to many people. It does not seem to matter greatly what the subject is, as long as the context is intimate and the story is told for its own sake, not forced to serve merely as the vehicle for an idea. The tone of the story need not be solemn. But I think intimacy is indispensable – a feeling that derives from a listener's trust and a storyteller's certain knowledge of his subject and regard for his audience. This intimacy deepens if the storyteller tempers his authority with humility, or when terms of idiomatic expression, or at least the physical setting for the story, are shared.

I THINK of two landscapes – one outside the self, the other within. The external landscape is the one we see – not only the line and color of the land and its shading at different times of the day, but also its plants and animals in season, its weather, its geology, the record of its climate and evolution. If you walk up, say, a dry arroyo in the Sonoran desert, you will feel a mounding and rolling of sand and silt beneath your foot that is distinctive. You will anticipate the crumbling of the sedimentary earth in the arroyo bank as your hand reaches out, and in that tangible evidence you will sense a history of water in the region. Perhaps a black-throated sparrow lands in a paloverde bush – the resiliency of the twig under the bird, that precise shade of yellowish-green against the milk-blue sky, the fluttering whir of the arriving sparrow, are what I mean by "the landscape." Draw on the smell of creosote bush, or clack stones together in the dry air. Feel how light is the desiccated dropping of the kangaroo rat. Study an animal track obscured by wind. These are all elements of the land, and what make the landscape comprehensible are the relationships between them. One learns a landscape finally not by knowing the name or identity of everything in it, but by perceiving the relationships in it – like that between the sparrow and the twig. The difference between the relationships and the elements is the same as that between written history and a catalogue of events.

The second landscape I think of is an interior one, a kind of projection within a person of a part of the exterior landscape. Relationships in the exterior landscape include those that are named and discernible, such as the nitrogen cycle, or a vertical

sequence of Ordovician limestone, and others that are uncodi-
fied or ineffable, such as winter light falling on a particular kind
of granite, or the effect of humidity on the frequency of a black-
poll warbler's burst of song. That these relationships have purpose and order, however inscrutable they may seem to us, is a
tenet of evolution. Similarly, the speculations, intuitions, and
formal ideas we refer to as "mind" are a set of relationships in
the interior landscape with purpose and order; some of these
are obvious, many impenetrably subtle. The shape and character of these relationships in a person's thinking, I believe, are
deeply influenced by where on this earth one goes, what one
touches, the patterns one observes in nature – the intricate history of one's life in the land, even a life in the city, where wind,
the chirp of birds, the line of a falling leaf, are known. These
thoughts are arranged, further, according to the thread of one's
moral, intellectual, and spiritual development. The interior
landscape responds to the character and subtlety of the exterior
one; the shape of the individual mind is affected by land as it
is by genes.

In stories like those I heard at Anaktuvuk Pass about wolverine, the relationship between separate elements in the land is
set forth clearly. It is put in a simple framework of sequential
incidents and apposite detail. If the exterior landscape is
limned well, the listener often feels that he has heard something pleasing and authentic – trustworthy. We derive this
sense of confidence, I think, not so much from verifiable truth
as from an understanding that lying has played no role in the
narrative. The storyteller is delegated to engage the reader
with a precise vocabulary, to set forth a coherent and dramatic
rendering of incidents – and to be ingenuous.

When one hears a story one takes pleasure in it for different
reasons – for the euphony of its phrases, an aspect of the plot,
or because one identifies with one of the characters. With certain stories certain individuals may experience a deeper, more
profound sense of well-being. This latter phenomenon, in my

understanding, rests at the heart of storytelling as an elevated experience among aboriginal peoples. It results from bringing the two landscapes together. The exterior landscape is organized according to principles or laws or tendencies beyond human control. It is understood to contain an integrity that is beyond human analysis and unimpeachable. Insofar as the storyteller depicts various subtle and obvious relationships in the exterior landscape accurately in his story, and insofar as he orders them along traditional lines of meaning to create the narrative, the narrative will "ring true." The listener who "takes the story to heart" will feel a pervasive sense of congruence within himself and also with the world.

Among the Navaho and, as far as I know, many other native peoples, the land is thought to exhibit a sacred order. That order is the basis of truth. Rituals themselves reveal the power in that order. Art, architecture, vocabulary, and costume, as well as ritual, derive from the perceived natural order of the universe – from observations and meditations on the exterior landscape. An indigenous philosophy – metaphysics, ethics, epistemology, æsthetics, and logic – may also derive from a people's contrived attentiveness to both the obvious (scientific) and ineffable (artistic) orders of the local landscape. Each individual, further, undertakes to order his interior landscape according to the exterior landscape. To succeed in this means to achieve a balanced state of mental health.

I think of the Navaho for a specific reason. Among the various sung ceremonies of this people – Enemyway, Coyoteway, Red Antway, Dogway – is one called Beautyway. In the Navaho view, the elements of one's interior life – one's psychological makeup and moral bearing – are subject to a persistent principle of disarray. Beautyway is, in part, a spiritual invocation of the order of the exterior universe, that irreducible, holy complexity that manifests itself as all things changing through time (a Navaho definition of beauty, hózhóó). The purpose of this invocation is to increase in the individual who is the subject of the Beautyway ceremony that same order, to make the individual again a reflection of the myriad enduring relationships of the landscape.

I BELIEVE STORY functions in a similar way. The purpose of storytelling is to achieve harmony between the two landscapes, to use all the elements – syntax, mood, figures of speech – in a harmonious way to reproduce the harmony of the land in the individual's interior. Inherent in story is the power to reorder a state of psychological confusion through contact with the pervasive truth of those relationships we call "the land."

These thoughts, of course, are susceptible to interpretation. I am convinced, however, that these observations can be applied to the kind of prose we call nonfiction as well as to traditional narrative forms such as the novel and the short story, and to some poems. Distinctions between fiction and nonfiction are sometimes obscured by arguments over what constitutes "the truth." In the aboriginal literature I am familiar with, the first distinction made among narratives is to separate the authentic from the inauthentic. Myth, which we tend to regard as fictitious or "merely metaphorical," is as authentic, as real, as the story of a wolverine in a man's lap. (A distinction is made, of course, about the elevated nature of myth – and frequently the circumstances of myth-telling are more rigorously prescribed than those for the telling of legends or vernacular stories – but all of these narratives are rooted in the local landscape. To violate *that* connection is to call the narrative itself into question.)

The power of narrative to nurture and heal, to repair a spirit in disarray, rests on two things: the skillful invocation of unimpeachable sources and the listener's knowledge that no hypocrisy or subterfuge is involved. This last simple fact is to me one of the most awesome aspects of the Holocene history of man.

WE ARE MORE accustomed now to thinking of "the truth" as something that can be explicitly stated, rather than as something that can be evoked in a metaphorical way outside science and Occidental culture. Neither can truth be reduced to aphorism or formulas. It is something alive and unpronounceable. Story creates a pattern in which it can reveal itself. For a storyteller to insist on relationships that do not exist is to lie. Lying is the opposite of story. (I do not mean to confuse ignorance with deception, or to imply that a storyteller can perceive all that is inherent in the land. Every storyteller falls short of a perfect limning of the landscape – perception and language both fail. But to make up something that is not there, something that can never be corroborated in the land, to knowingly set forth a false relationship, is to be lying, no longer telling a story.)

Because of the intricate, complex nature of the land, it is not always possible for a storyteller to grasp what is contained in a story. The intent of the storyteller, then, must be to evoke, honestly, some single aspect of all that the land contains. The storyteller knows that because different individuals grasp the story at different levels, the focus of his regard for truth must be at the primary one – with who was there, what happened, when, where, and why things occurred. The story will then possess similar truth at other levels – the integrity inherent at the primary level of meaning will be conveyed everywhere else. As long as the storyteller accurately describes the order before him, it is even possible for the story to be more successful than the storyteller himself is able to imagine.

I would like to make a final point about the wolverine stories I heard at Anaktuvuk Pass. I wrote down the details afterward, concentrating especially on aspects of the biology and ecology of the animals. I sent the information on to my friend living with the Cree. When, many months later, I saw him, I asked whether the Cree had enjoyed these insights of the Nunamiut into the nature of the wolverine. What had they said?

"You know," he told me, "how they are. They said, 'That *could* happen.'"

In these uncomplicated words the Cree announced their own knowledge of the wolverine. They acknowledged that although they themselves had never seen the things the Nunamiut spoke of, they accepted them as accurate observations, because they did not consider storytelling a context for misrepresentation. They also preserved their own dignity by not overstating their confidence in the Nunamiut, a distant and unknown people.

Whenever I think of this courtesy on the part of the Cree, I think of the dignity that is ours when we cease to demand the truth and realize that the best we can have of those substantial truths that guide our lives is metaphorical – a story. And the most of it we are likely to discern comes only when we accord one another the respect the Cree showed the Nunamiut. Beyond this – that truth reveals itself most fully not in dogma but in the paradox, irony, and contradictions that distinguish compelling narratives – beyond this there are only failures of imagination: reductionism in science; fundamentalism in religion; fascism in politics.

Our national literatures should be important to us insofar as they sustain us with illumination and heal us. They can always do that so long as they are written with an understanding of why the human heart and the land have been brought together so regularly in human history.

RICHARD FORD

�֍

The Three Kings: Hemingway, Faulkner, and Fitzgerald

SOME BOYS, alas, do not come to serious reading, nor God knows to serious writing, precisely like hounds to round steak. Though, then again, special boys sometimes do.

I remember a few years ago reading in *Exile's Return*, Malcolm Cowley's wonderful book on the Twenties, the teenage correspondence between Cowley and Kenneth Burke. It is pretentious, chin-pulling stuff sent from Burke's parents' apartment in Weehawken to Cowley's house in Pittsburgh, dwelling chiefly on whatever were the palmy literary aspirations just then dawning on those two little booksniffs. It was 1915. Cowley was just leaving for Harvard, having already, he boasted, banged through Kipling, Congreve, and Conrad, plus a dozen other of the greats. Burke — poet and teacher to be — was contemplating his first grand tour of France, rhapsodizing about how much he loved the moon and all those things that didn't fit him out for literature, while advertising himself as "somewhat of an authority on unpresentable French novels" and the lesser Chopin — altogether things that they must both blush at now. But still, I thought: What smart boys they were! And what remarkable letters! They had already read more, I realized, digested it better, gotten it down for quicker recall, and were putting it to fancier uses at seventeen than all I'd read, understood, remembered, or could hope to make use of to that very moment. Or maybe ever. And my hat was, and continues to be, off to them.

Until I entered college at Michigan State, where I'd come from Mississippi in 1962 to learn to be a hotel manager, my own reading had been chiefly of the casual drugstore and cereal box type. Whatever came easy. And what *I* was doing when I wasn't reading Congreve or Kipling or Faulkner, Hemingway, or Fitzgerald at an early and seasoning age was whirling crazy around Mississippi in a horrible flat-black '57 Ford Fairlane my grandparents had bought me; fecklessly swiping hubcaps and occasionally cars, going bird hunting on posted land with my buddy-pals, snarfling schoolgirls, sneaking into drive-ins, drinking, fighting, and generally entertaining myself fatherlessly in the standard American ways – ways Cowley and Burke never write about that I've seen, and so probably knew little about firsthand.

Though, in truth, my "preparation" strikes me as the more usual American one, starting off from that broad middle ground between knowing nothing and knowing a little *about* something. Conceivably it is the very plane Faulkner and Fitzgerald and Hemingway themselves started out from at my age, or a couple of years younger – not particularly proud of their ignorance, but not sufficiently daunted by it to keep them (and me) from barging off toward appealing and unfamiliar terrains. They were novelists, after all, not experts in literature. And what they wrote about was people living ordinary lives for which history had not quite readied them. And it is, I think, a large part of why we like them so much when we read them. They were like us. And what they wrote about reminded us of ourselves and sanctioned our lives.

Reading was, in truth, my very problem in Mississippi. While I always read faster and with more "comprehension" than my school grade was supposed to (I used to pride myself, in the tenth grade, that I could read as well as any Ole Miss freshman), I was still slow, slow. Slow as Christmas. And I am still slow, though more practiced now. I have thought that had I been evaluated by today's standards, I'd have been deemed a special student and held back. Whereas in Mississippi, 1960, I was decidedly college prep.

I have also realized, since then, that I may well and only have changed from hotel management to the study of literature in college not so much because I loved literature – what did I know? – but because it was a discipline for the slow (i.e., careful). And I'll admit as well that at Michigan State knowing about Faulkner, Hemingway, and Fitzgerald, which I began to do that first year, was a novelty to set one comfortably and creditably apart from one's fraternity brothers from Menomonie and Ishpeming, who by that time were already sunk greedy-deep into packaging engineering, retailing theory, and hotel management – all those necessary arts and sciences for which Michigan State has become justly famous.

I REMEMBER very distinctly the first time I read anything by F. Scott Fitzgerald. I read the story "Absolution," in my first English literature class at MSU. It was 1962. And I remember it distinctly because it was the first story assigned for class, and because I didn't understand anything that happened in it.

"Absolution" was written by Fitzgerald in 1924, when he was twenty-seven, hardly older than I was when I read it. In it, a fantasizing little Minnesota schoolboy lies in Holy Confession, then gets mistakenly forced to take Communion with an impure soul. Later, and in a state of baleful terror, the boy – Rudolph Miller – confesses what he's done to the same priest, who absolves him peevishly, only then promptly and in Rudolph's presence suffers his own spiritual crack-up, giving up his senses to a giddy rhapsody about glimmering merry-go-rounds and shining, dazzling strangers – all, we suppose, because he'd done nothing more venturesome than be a priest all his life. Little Rudolph sits by horrified. But in his wretchedness he has figured out already that private acts of pride and comfort matter more than public ones of abstraction and pretense. And while the priest writhes on the floor, howling like a lunatic, Rudolph slips away, having acknowledged something mysterious and consequential that will last him all his life.

End of story.

It is one of Fitzgerald's very best; youthful innocence brought into the alembic of a tawdry, usurping experience. A genuine rite of passage. Real drama.

I did not understand it because even though my mother had been a convent girl in Ft. Smith, still occasionally sat in on masses, and, I believe, wished all her life and secretly that she could be a Catholic instead of a married-over Presbyterian, I did not know what absolution meant.

That is, I did not know what the word meant, and indeed what all the trouble was about. A considerable impediment.

Nor was I about to look it up. I was not big on looking things up then. It could've been that I had heard of F. Scott Fitzgerald before. Though I don't know why I would have. He was not from Mississippi. But you could argue that Americans up to a certain age, and at that particular time, were simply born knowing who F. Scott Fitzgerald was. Ernest Hemingway and William Faulkner, too. It's possible they were just in the American air. And once we breathed that air, we knew something.

It is also true that if I knew *about* F. Scott Fitzgerald – likewise Hemingway and Faulkner – before I knew them hands-on, through direct purchase of their published work, say for instance, as I had read hungrily through some Mississippi dowager's private stacks, opened to the bookless boy who craved to read and to learn (the way it happens in French biographies, though not in mine), it is because by that time, 1961-62, all three were already fully apotheosized; brought up to a plane of importance important Americans always seem to end up on: as celebrities, estranged from the rare accomplishments that first earned them notice.

What I didn't know, though, was what absolution meant, nor anything much of what that story was about. If I had, it might've changed my life, might've signaled me how to get along better with my own devious prides and festerings. But I was just too neck-up then in my own rites of passage to acknowledge anybody else's. And while I may even have known what that expression meant, I couldn't fathom the one Fitzgerald was writing about.

So my first experience with him gave me this: Puzzlement. Backed up by a vague, free-floating self-loathing, I was, after all, not very studious then, and I balanced that habit with a vast ignorance I was not aware of. I was pledging Sigma Chi at the same time.

I KNOW I knew who William Faulkner was by at least 1961. He *was* from Mississippi. Though I had not read a word he'd written about it. When I got to Michigan State, though, he immediately became part of the important territory I was staking out for myself. He, and Ross Barnett, and a kind of complex, swinish liberalness I affected to keep black guys from stomping on me on general principle.

I *had* laid eyes on William Faulkner. At the Alumni House at Ole Miss in the fall in 1961. Or at least I remember thinking I had. And in any case I certainly told people at Michigan State I had – tightening my grip on things rightly mine. But I know I had never read anything of his, or even of Eudora Welty's – who lived only a few blocks from me and whom I used to see buying her lunch at the steam table at the Jitney Jungle grocery, where our families shopped, but never bothered to inquire about, though her niece, Elizabeth, was in my class.

I had, by the time I left high school, strangely enough, read Geoffrey Chaucer. He was unavoidable in senior English. I could (and still can) recite from memory the first fourteen lines of the Prologue to *The Canterbury Tales*, in Middle English, without giving one thought to what any of it signifies.

I had also "written" a term paper on Thomas Wolfe by then, though I hadn't read a word he'd written either. I had been given Andrew Turnbull's biography of Wolfe and had boosted most of my text straight from there, verbatim and unconsidered. I got a B.

I do remember, somewhere in this period, noticing that a friend of mine, Frank Newell, had a copy of *The Wild Palms*. It was on his bookshelf at home, in the old green-tinted and lurid Random House dust jacket with the pastel wild palms on it. I thought that Frank Newell's family were literary people because of that. And I thought *The Wild Palms* was probably a novel about Florida. In a year I would read my first Faulkner, in the same English class in college: "A Rose for Emily." And I liked it immensely. But I was surprised to know Faulkner wrote some scary stories. Somehow I had expected something different from a man who'd won the Nobel Prize.

AS FOR HEMINGWAY, I remember that best of all. I knew who he was by at least 1960, when I was sixteen, because my mother liked him. That is, she liked *him*.

I, of course, had not read a word, and I can't be absolutely certain my mother had, though she was a reader. Books like *The Egg and I* and *Lydia Bailey* went around our house in Mississippi, and we both had put in a lot of time in the Jackson Public Library, where it was either cool or warm at the right times of the year and where I would browse in comfort through the *National Geographic*s.

What she liked about Hemingway was, I think, the way he looked. His picture had been in *Life* or *Look* in the Fifties, looking about like the Karsh photo that's still sometimes seen in magazines. A rough yet sensitive guy. A straight-talking man of letters in a fisherman's sweater. The right look.

She also liked something he'd said in public about dying, about how dying wasn't so bad but living with death till it indignified you was poison, and how he would take his own life when that happened to him, which I guess he did. That my mother liked, too. She kept the quotation on a three-by-five card, written in her own hand, stuck inside the phone book, where I would occasionally see it and feel craven embarrassment. She admired resolution and certainty about first principles. And so, I suppose, did I, though not with enough interest to hunt up a novel of Hemingway's and see what else there was to it. This was about the time my father died of a heart attack, at home, in my arms and in her presence. And we – she and I – became susceptible to certain kinds of rigor as stanches against grief and varieties of bad luck. For a while during this period she kept company with a big, burly-bluff guy named Matt, who was married and drove a powerful car and carried a .45 caliber pistol strapped to the steering column (I liked him very much) and who growled when he talked and who might've seemed like Hemingway to someone who knew absolutely nothing about him, but who had a notion.

In any case, though, my mother, who was born in northwest Arkansas, in a dirt-floor cabin near the Oklahoma line and the Osage Strip, and who has now died, was, importantly, the first person I knew of who was truly Hemingwayesque. And that included Ernest Hemingway himself.

These, then, were the first writers' names to be chalked, if obscurely, onto my remarkably clean slate, a fact vouched true to me by my ability to remember when I knew of them and by my dead reckoning that before that time I knew of no writers at all – except Geoffrey Chaucer and a part of Andrew Turnbull that I stole. I arrived at 1962, the year I would first read William Faulkner, Scott Fitzgerald, and Ernest Hemingway, remarkably ignorant for a boy of eighteen; as unlettered, in fact, as a porch monkey, and without much more sense than that idle creature of what literature was good for, or to what uses it might be put in my life. Not at all a writer. And not one bit the seasoned, reasonable, apprentice bookman customary to someone who before long would want to be a novelist.

For these three kings, then, a kingdom was vacant.

A<small>ND SO</small> I read them, badly. At least at first.

It was in the dog days of the New Criticism that I read *The Sun Also Rises*, *Absalom! Absalom!*, and *The Great Gatsby*. We were being instructed to detect literature's most intrinsic worth by holding its texts aloof from life and history, and explicating and analyzing its parts to pieces. Close reading, this was known as. And my professors – one, a bemused, ex-second-string football player from Oregon; and the other, a gentle, strange-suited, bespectacled man with the picturesque, Hemingway name of Sam Baskett – put us through our formalist/objectivist paces like dreary drill sergeants. Point of view. Dramatic structure. Image. Theme. Hemingway and Faulkner were still alive at that time, and Fitzgerald managed somehow to retain his contemporariness. And there was, among us students, a fine, low-grade brio that here we were reading new work. Probably my teachers admired these men's writing. Generationally they were much more under the thumb of their influence than I could ever be, and possibly they had wanted to be writers themselves once. (One told me that people who wanted to be writers should take jobs as fire watchers and live alone in towers.) But they still chose to teach literature to satisfy a weary system, and in any case it was in these dry classroom anatomies that I first learned exactly what meaning meant.

Symbols, I remember, were very much on my teachers' minds then, and so on mine. I was not yet *reading like a writer*. Indeed, I was just learning to read like a reader – still slowly – so that I never really got onto the symbol business as straight as I might've. But we Jessie Weston'ed the daylights out of poor Hemingway and Fitzgerald; unearthed wastelands, identified penises, fish, and fisher kings all over everywhere. From my sad underlinings and margin notes of that time, I can see that Dr. T. J. Eckleburg, the brooding, signboard optometrist, was very important to my reading of *The Great Gatsby*. He meant God, fate, decadence, evil and impotence, and was overlord of the wasteland – all qualities and identities I could not make fit together, since they seemed like different things, and since my sense of meaning dictated that assignments only be made one to one.

Jake Barnes's mystery war wound likewise supplied me no end of industry. For a time everyone in that book was wounded, or at least alienated very badly. Many things are marked "Ironic." Many things are marked "Imp." And everywhere I could I underlined *rod, bull, bandillera, worm,* and noted "Symb."

Of course, I paid no special attention to the lovely, lyrical celebration of comradeship among Jake and Bill and the Englishman, Harris, there on the Irati – a passage I now think of as the most sweetly moving and meaningful in the novel. Nor to the passage in *Gatsby* where Nick tries to say how Gatsby must've felt at the sad end of things, when he had "paid a high price for living too long with a single dream." I suppose I was just too young for all that, too busy making things harder, getting my ducks set in a straight row.

This, as I've said, was around the time I read "Absolution," and was completely puzzled by it. I was not, however, puzzled by Faulkner, whose gravity and general profusion so daunted the Michiganders I sat beside in class, since he resisted our New Critical shakedown like a demon. There was really just too much of everything in *Absalom! Absalom!* Life, in words, geysering and eddying over each other, so that just being sure what was what and who was who became challenge enough to make you beg off choosing among what things might formally *mean* – a valuable enough lesson, certainly for anyone who wants to learn about anything, ever.

Faulkner dazzled me, of course, as his writing inevitably will. But being from where he was from, I was already acquainted with the way the white man's peculiar experience in that particular locale over time begot the need to tell; to rehearse, explain, twist, revise, and alibi life clear out of its own weirdness and paradox and eventually into a kind of fulgent, cumulative, and acceptable sense. Begot, in fact, so much larruping and fabricating that language somehow became paramount for its own sake (a fresh idea to me) and in turn begot its own irony, its own humors, and genealogy and provenance.

That, I came to understand, was meaning, too.

For me, reading Faulkner was like coming upon a great iridescent glacier that I had dreamed about. I may have been daunted by the largeness and gravity and variety of what he told. But he never puzzled me so as to make me feel ignorant, as I had been before I read him, or when I read "Absolution." To the contrary. When I read *Absalom! Absalom!* those years ago, everything came *in* to me. I got something. Somehow the literal sense of all I did and didn't understand, laid in the caress of those words – all of it, absolutely commensurate with life – suddenly seemed a pleasure, not a task. And I loved it.

Before, I don't believe I'd known what made literature necessary; neither what quality of life required that it be represented, nor what quality in literature made such abstractings a good idea. In other words, the singular value of written words, and their benefit to lived life, had not been impressed on me. That is, until I read *Absalom! Absalom!*, which, among other things, sets out to testify by act to the efficacy of telling, and to recommend language for its powers of consolation against whatever's ailing you.

I point this out now because if anything I read influenced me to take a try at being a writer – even on a midget scale – it was this pleasure I got from reading Faulkner. I wrote my first story about this time, a moody, inconclusive, not especially Faulkner-like domestic minidrama called "Saturday," which I liked. And putting those events together makes me understand now how much the wish to trade in language as a writer traces to a pleasure gotten from its use as a reader.

Not that it has to be that way. For some writers I'm sure ideas come first. For others, pictures. For others, probably symbols and Vico. But for me it was telling, in words. I don't think I ever read the same way after that but began to read, in my own way, like a writer. Not to satisfy a system, but to take whatever pleasure there was from language, no matter what I under-

stood or could parse. And that, I am satisfied now, is the way
one should always read. At least to start.

In the spring of 1964, my wife and I – barely not children
and certainly not yet married – drove in an old Chrysler north
from East Lansing up into the lake counties where most of
Hemingway's Michigan stories are set – Charlevoix, Emmet,
Mackinac. The two of us hiked around sunny days through East
Jordan and Petoskey, picnicked on beaches where the rich Chi-
cagoans used to come summers, boated on Walloon Lake,
staying in a little matchstick motel across the straits in St. Ignace
just to say we'd been there and seen the bridge that wasn't there
when Hemingway wrote about the country.

   Though I was there to get a closer, more personal lowdown
on those stories; stories I had been reading that spring, had
loved on instinct, felt intensely, but that had also sparked my
first honest act of literary criticism: namely, that I felt they
never *ever* quite said enough. They forbore too much, skimped
on language, made too much of silences. As if things were
said only for the gods, and the gods didn't tolerate that much.
And I was there, I suppose, curious and nervous about silences, to tune in on things with some experience of my own.
It seems romantic now. And it probably *was* silly. But it was my
way of taking things seriously and to heart. My way of reading.

   What I didn't understand, of course, and certainly didn't
learn marching around those woods fifty years too late, was that
these were a young man's stories. And their severe economies – I
think of "Indian Camp," because it was my special favorite –
were the economies and silences of a still limited experience,
an intelligence that wasn't finished yet, though certainly also a
talent masterful at mining feelings with words, or at least at the
nervy business of stripping words in such a pattern as to strand
the feelings nicely inside the limits of the story.

It was a young man's æsthetic, and ideal for impressing another young man.

But I wanted badly to know why that Indian had killed himself! And I did not understand why Nick's father wouldn't just come out, while they were heading home in the boat, and say it. Tell us. Telling was what writing did, I thought. And I wasn't savvy enough myself *not* to be told. Faulkner would've told it. He'd have had Judge Benbow or Rosa Coldfield spill it out. Fitzgerald would've had somebody try to explain later on, in another city in the Middle West.

Hemingway, though, was after something he thought was purer. Later, I read in *Death in the Afternoon* that he aimed for the "sequence of motion and fact which made the emotion." Whereas, if you said a thing—explained it—you could lose it, which is what Jake Barnes says. And indeed what you lost was the feeling of the thing, the feeling of awe, terror, loss. Think of "Hills Like White Elephants," a story I admire and that students love because it seems so modern. No one says *abortion* in it. Yet the feeling of abortion—loss, puzzlement, abstraction—informs every slender, stylized gesture and line, and the story has a wonderful effect.

But the embryo writer in me, even then, wanted more. More language spent. More told so that I could know more of what went on there and feel it in the plush of the words. A man had died. And I wanted the risk the other way, risking the "blur" Hemingway so distrusted—an effect caused by a writer who has not seen something "clearly," yet who still needs to get at a truth by telling it. The world, for me, even back in 1964, seemed too various, too full, and literature too resourceful to draw such rigid lines about life just to preserve a feeling.

To me, Hemingway kept secrets rather than discovered them. He held the overcomplex world too much at arm's length either because he wouldn't on principle or couldn't say more. And for that reason I distrusted him. He valued accuracy and precision over truth, and for that reason, despite his effects, he seemed a specialist in what he himself called "minor passions." Even today, when I am always surprised at how much broader a writer he is than I remember, he still seems like a high school team captain with codes, a man who peaked too early and never went on to greater, harder feats.

Not, of course, that I didn't take with me something valuable from Hemingway, namely a deference for genuine mystery. I may now know what absolution means and why the Indian kills himself – too many doctors, too much pain and indignity. I may know beyond much doubt what was Jake Barnes's wound. But I also learned that for anyone, at any time, some things that matter can't be told, either because they're too important or too hard to bring to words, and these things can be the subject of stories. I think I learned that first and best reading Hemingway, learned the manners and protocols and codes a story observes when it comes round something it thinks is a consequential mystery. I may still prefer that mystery, once broached, be an inducement, not a restraint, to language, a signal to imagination to begin saying whatever can be said. But to have learned of that mystery at an early age is no small thing. And my debt for it is absolute.

From this highly reactive time, my memories of Fitzgerald are, at best, indistinct. I made my way through *The Great Gatsby*, exclusively settling matters of point of view and Dr. Eckleburg's significations. Then I simply left off, my memory retaining only the faraway beacon light on Daisy Buchanan's boat dock (it was "Imp."), and Gatsby floating dead in his swimming pool, a memory I soon confused with the beginning of the movie *Sunset Boulevard*, in which the corpse played by William Holden, not Nick Carraway, tells the story.

What I *was* attentive to, though, in my bird dog's way, were the subliterate runs and drumbeats of words, their physical and auditory manifestations, the extremes of utterance and cadence, what Sartre called the *outside* of language. It is undoubtedly one reason I liked Faulkner best, since he offers so much to the poorly educated but overly sensitized.

And my belief was that these etherish matters were matters

of literary style. And like all novices, I became preoccupied with that.

What followed, then, was a partitioning up of literature into Faulkneresque and Hemingwayesque, leaving a kind of stylistic no-man's-land for all the other people. To me, Fitzgerald, by having the softest drumbeats, the fewest linguistic extremes and quirks, the rarest ethers, didn't really seem to have much of a style, or if he did he had a poor, thin one.

It seems feasible that one could think that putting Fitzgerald midway between the great putter-inner and the great taker-outer casts a kind of convenient cosmos map of the male soul and its choices. Though what I was doing twenty years ago, when I was almost twenty, was just confusing style with idiosyncrasy and making myself its champion.

Not that it was entirely my fault.

My ex-quarterback of a professor (we'd heard he'd played behind Terry Baker, and so had had plenty of time for reading) had assigned us all to write a paragraph in either "the style of Hemingway" or "the style of Faulkner" — a miserable, treacherous task to assign any student, but particularly to one who had begun to write. (Though I now understand it was designed chiefly to kill class time.)

But we all wrote. And when we read our paragraphs aloud, mine produced the profoundest response from my instructor. He stopped me three sentences in and complained to all that my Hemingway sounded like everybody else's Faulkner, and that I clearly was not much good for this kind of thing.

I was badly stung. I liked style, whatever it was. And I believed I could be its master. Only I saw I needed to study it harder — Hemingway and Faulkner in particular, and what was so odd about them that I couldn't imitate them separately.

Nobody, though, was asking me to write a paragraph in the style of Fitzgerald at this time. *Fitzgeraldian* was not a word. And so for this reason he fell even more completely below my notice.

It is notable to me that somewhere in this period someone placed in my hands, for reasons I do not remember, a copy of

Arthur Mizener's gossipy, pseudo-scholarly biography of Fitzgerald, *The Far Side of Paradise*, the edition with the Van Vechten
photo on the front, a smiling, wide-faced Fitzgerald practically
unrecognizable from the Princetonian-Arrow shirt profile on
the Scribner's books.

Reading Mizener was a big mistake for me. His biographer's
interest was the archly anti-New Critical one of mutually cor-
roborating art and life. And since Fitzgerald, at least for a time,
had lived a very, very *rich* life, there set on for me a long period
in which I could not distinguish accurately all he'd done from
all that he'd written: the profligacy, the madness, the high style
and helling around, ruinous wives, prep schools, the Plaza,
Princeton, New York, Paris, Minnesota, Hollywood. I read the
other novels, the stories and notebooks. And though I didn't
exactly forget them, they just fell to his life. *He* seemed smart
and too clever and poignant and overweening. But the books
almost always faded back into Fitzgerald myth, into imputation,
half-fact, lie, remembrance, and confession – annals where
even now for me they have their truest resonance.

Today, I still believe it's as much his failure as mine that I remember as much about him as I do, but can sort out so little of
his work. And that his life – vulnerable, exemplary, short writer's
life – save for a brilliant novel and a few excellent short pieces,
makes a better story. It is tempting to think that, like Dick Diver
and Amory Blaine and Anthony Patch, he represents some
promising but spoilable part of our American self-conception.
And since that is not exactly tragic, it is maybe more appealing
and exemplary to us as biography than illusion.

Recently I read *The Great Gatsby* again, for possibly the fourth
time (I know people who brag they read it every year). Fitzgerald wrote it before he was thirty, and as I get older it only gets
better. I believe it is one of the maturest, more sophisticated
and seamless books I have read, and I don't fault myself for not
getting it back in 1964, since it has, I think, more to teach an
older man than a young one.

And I have found its style: its elegant economies and proportionings, the sleek trajectory of its complex little story, the strategy of withholding Gatsby until his place is set, Fitzgerald's certain eye for the visual detail and, once observed, for that detail's suitability as host for his wonderful, clear judgment about Americans and American life – a judgment, Wilson said, "saturated with twentieth-century America."

The essence of Fitzgerald's style finally was that he itched to say something smart on the page, and made his novels accommodate that. It is why as a young man he was always better in shorter, manageable forms, and why a savvy young man might've learned plenty from him without ever having to mimic. And it is why I had such a hard time at first, my own ear then being chiefly to the ground.

Faulkner, of course, was the best of all three, and the very best of any American writing fiction in this century. It is not even discredit to Hemingway and Fitzgerald to say so. Liking Faulkner or not liking him is akin to liking or not liking the climate in some great territorial expanse. It seems like tautology. Whereas Hemingway and Fitzgerald, I sense, come to our affections more like the weather does, passingly.

No writer, including Henry James, minted more robust characters freshly and indelibly into our American literary memory. All those Snopeses, Temple Drake, Thomas Sutpen, Benjy Compson, Dilsey. A bear. No writer has exceeded his own natural regionalism (that dark American literary peril), or survived the codification of his style, or confessed apparently less of his personal life as grandly as Faulkner has. No one braves as much in a sentence. No one is as consistently or boisterously funny as Faulkner while remaining serious and dramatic. And, of course, no American writer this century has been so influential – impressive is the best word – both in the restraining effects of his work on other writers, and in the most generous ways as well: his work always urges all of us if not to be more hopeful, at least to be more various, to include more, see more, say more that is hopeful and surprising and humorous and that is true.

I loved Faulkner when I read him first. He stumped the sym-
bolizers, the mythologizers, the taxonomists, the *pov* guys dead
in the brackets in East Lansing. He would not reduce so as to
mean more. And that I liked.

Though it seemed to me, then, as it did ten years later when
I was writing a novel set in Mississippi – my home too – that
that was because he'd appropriated everything there was. It was
even possible to want to write like Faulkner without knowing
you did; to want to put down some sense of a life there without
realizing it existed first in his sentences. Until the end of the Fifties – 1963 – I am convinced, a large part of *everybody's* idea of
the South came from William Faulkner, whether they'd read
him or not. He was in the American air, as I said before. And
that went for the air southerners breathed too, since we could
see how right he'd gotten it, and since, of course, he was ours.

How can I measure what it was worth to read Hemingway,
Fitzgerald, and Faulkner back then in the Sixties? Influence on
a writer is a hard business to assess, and I'm not sure I would
tell the truth if I could, since real influence means being affected by the weather in another writer's sentences, sometimes
so much that you can't even imagine writing except in that
weather. And no one who's any good ever wants to write like
anyone else.

One truth is that my generation of writers – born mostly in
the Forties – has not lived "the same life, the generic one" that
Lowell speaks about in his elegy for his friend John Berryman.
We have not all prized or even read the same books. We have
not all had or aspired to teaching jobs. We do not all know one
another. Lowell, of course, was probably wrong about his generation, since, from what I can tell of his thinking, it included
only about fifteen people. But of my own, I am sure we are too
many, too spread out and differently inclined ever to have been
influenced similarly by another generation's writers.

Another truth is that I don't remember a lot of those books

anymore. And I never read them all to start with. A fellow I met recently, who had spent time in a North Vietnamese prison, asked me if I thought Francis Macomber's wife shot him on purpose. And I had no idea. In my mind I had confused that story with *The Snows of Kilimanjaro*, and when I went back to figure out the answer, I was surprised. (Of course, Hemingway being Hemingway, I'm still not 100 percent sure what happened.)

Likewise, when I began to think on this essay, I chose a Faulkner novel just to graze over for atmosphere, one I thought I hadn't read – *Sanctuary* – but knew to be easy because of what Faulkner had written about it. Only now that I've finished it, I really can't be certain if I'd read it years ago or not. Odd. But there you are.

Still, as a little group, they seem to have traversed the Sixties and Seventies intact, despite the fact of a unique and intense war's being on then, and of immediate life's altering so rapidly and irrevocably. To me, they seem far away, their writing become *literature* finally. But that is only because I don't read them so much, and when I do it is usually to teach readers who were being born just when Hemingway and Faulkner were dying.

Though *their* pleasure seems certain.

I have always assigned classes to read "Babylon Revisited," Fitzgerald's bitter, touching story about Charlie Wales, the man who comes to Paris to reclaim his daughter, lost to him by the calamities of the Twenties, and the Crash, and by his own bad luck and improvidence. It is one of my favorite stories. And there is always a sentiment among students that it keeps its currency because of the Thirties' similarities – at least in my students' minds – to those years since the Sixties were over.

Faulkner still seems to excite the awe and affection he excited in me, though no one – correctly – wants to write like him. Only Hemingway, I detect, can occasionally exert a genuine and direct influence on young writers' "style." His old, dour, at-war-with-words correctness seems to ride the waves of austerity, ascending in tough, Republican times, and declining when life seems abler to support grand illusions.

As writers whose work taught me serviceable lessons about writing at a formative age, all three get high marks for mentorship – a role Hemingway cared much to fill, and that Faulkner, if we take to heart the sarcasm of his Nobel address, probably thought was ridiculous.

By 1968, when I had started graduate school in California, people were still talking about Faulkner, Hemingway, and Fitzgerald, though primarily just as Dutch uncles to our own newborn artistic credos. We were all tiny savages then, trying on big boys' clothes. Though it was still good to be able to quote a particular novel – *As I Lay Dying* was popular – or to own something specific one of them had reportedly said and be able to unsheathe it fast. *The Crack-Up* was highly prized as a *vade mecum*, along with the *Paris Review* interviews and *A Moveable Feast*.

Anyone who actually *wrote* like Faulkner or Hemingway was, of course, thought to be washed up from the start. But with their books, others' faults could be neatly exposed, crow and humble pie served to order. We were being read to by Richard Brautigan, taught by E. L. Doctorow, and imitating Donald Barthelme. But we were still interested in how those older men got along in the world where there were no grants or teaching jobs, and how they acted out their parts. One fellow in my class actually asked us all to call him Papa. And when I remember that, I need no better proof that they were in our lives, still behind us all, like Mount Rushmore in the Santa Ana hills.

Speaking selectively, I know I learned from the economies of *The Great Gatsby* how to get on with things narrative; how to get people in and out of scenes and doors and sections of the country by seizing some showy detail and then going along to whatever was next.

From Hemingway I learned just how little narrative "instrusion" (we talked that way) was actually necessary to keep the action going, and I also learned to value the names of things, and to try to know how things worked as a way of dominating life and perfecting its illusion. There was, as well, the old workshop rapier that said Hemingway's famous dialogue, when actually spoken aloud, sounded like nothing more than an angry robot on Valium, and not like real talk. Yet locked within is the greater lesson that the page is officially different from the life, and that in creating life's illusion, the page need not exactly mimic – need not nearly mimic, really – and, moreover, that this very discrepancy is what sets art free.

From Faulkner I'm sure I learned that in "serious" fiction it is possible to be funny at the expense of nothing – a lesson also discernible in Shakespeare; that it is sometimes profitable to take risks with syntax and diction, and bring together words that ordinarily do not seem to belong together – the world being not completely foregone – and in this small way reinvent the language and cause pleasure. And finally, from Faulkner, that in representing life one needs to remember that many, many things do not stand to reason.

They were all three dead, of course, before I had written a word. Already kings. But still, I and my generation might have learned from them just what time in life our words could start to mean something to someone else – nervy business, when you think of it. They all wrote brilliant books in their twenties. We might also have learned that great literature can sometimes be written by amateurs who are either smart enough or sufficiently miscast to need to take their personal selves very seriously. In this way we might've learned some part of what talent is.

And last, we might've learned from them that the only real *place* for a writer in this country is at the top of the heap. That the only really satisfactory sanction available, the one our parents could appreciate as happily as the occupations they wanted for us – the law and banking – is success, and the personal price for success is sometimes very high, and is almost always worth it.

WHAT I REMEMBER of them, though, is something else again, different from what they taught me. Though by saying what I actually remember, or some of it, I may say best why for me and possibly for people like me, they are three kings.

I remember, for instance, what Nick Carraway said about all our personalities, and Gatsby's in particular: that they are only "an unbroken series of successful gestures."

I remember that Hemingway gave up his first good wife, and never forgave himself for it, and that Fitzgerald kept his until she helped ruin him. (On the eve of my marriage I remember asking my soon-to-be-wife to please read *The Beautiful and the Damned*, and to promise not to ruin me in that particular way.)

I remember Hemingway saying, "It is certainly valuable to a trained writer to crash in an airplane that burns."

I remember Darl Bundren in *As I Lay Dying*, describing his sister Dewey Dell's breasts as "mammalian ludicrosities which are the horizons and valleys of the earth."

I remember Horace Benbow saying to a man already doomed, "You're not being tried by common sense....You're being tried by a jury."

I remember where I learned what a bota bag was and how it was used – important gear for a fraternity man.

I remember where I learned what it meant to have *repose* – *Tender Is the Night* – and that I didn't have it.

I remember that dead Indian very distinctly.

I remember what Fitzgerald said – sounding more like Hemingway than our version of Fitzgerald, but really speaking for all three writers – that "Life was something you dominated, if you were any good."

And last, I remember what Fitzgerald wrote in his notebook about Dick Diver: "He looked like me."

This is the important stuff of my memory: objects, snapshots, odd despairs, jokes, instructions, codes. Plain life charted through its middle grounds. Literature put to its best uses. The very thing I didn't know when I started.

These men were literalists, though they could be ironic. They were writers of reference. They were intuitors and observers of small things for larger purposes. They were not zealots, nor politicians. Not researchers nor experts nor experimenters. They seemed to come to us one to one. And though Faulkner could seem difficult, really he was not if you relented as I did.

Their work, in other words, seemed like *real* work, and we gave up disbelief without difficulty and said willingly, "This is our writing." They wrote to bring the news. And they were wondrous at that task. They wrote a serious, American literature that a boy who had read nothing could read to profit, and then read for the rest of his life.

"You've got to sell your heart," Fitzgerald said, and write "so that people can read it blind like braille." And in a sense, with their work they sold their hearts for us, and that inspires awe and fear and even pity. Reverence suitable for kings.

GRETEL EHRLICH

✖

Looking for a Lost Dog

The most valuable thoughts which I entertain are anything
but what *I* thought. Nature abhors a vacuum, and if I can
only walk with sufficient carelessness I am sure to be filled.
                                —HENRY DAVID THOREAU

I STARTED OFF this morning looking for my lost dog. He's a
red heeler, blotched brown and white, and I tell people he looks
like a big saddle shoe. Born at Christmas on a thirty-below-zero
night, he's tough, though his right front leg is crooked where
it froze to the ground.

It's the old needle-in-the-haystack routine: small dog, huge
landscape, and rugged terrain. While moving cows once, he fell
in a hole and disappeared. We heard him whining but couldn't
see him. When we put our ears to the ground, we could hear
the hole that had swallowed him.

It's no wonder human beings are so narcissistic. The way our
ears are constructed, we can only hear what's right next to us
or else the internal monologue inside. I've taken to cupping
my hands behind my ears — mule-like — and pricking them all
the way forward or back to hear what's happened or what's
ahead.

"Life is polyphonic," a Hungarian friend in her eighties said.
She was a child prodigy from Budapest who had soloed on the
violin in Paris and Berlin by the time she was twelve. "Childish-
ly, I once thought hearing had mostly to do with music," she

said. "Now that I'm too old to play the fiddle, I know it has to do with the great suspiration of life everywhere."

But back to the dog. I'm walking and looking and listening for him, though there is no trail, no clue, no direction to the search. Whimsically, I head north toward the falls. They're set in a deep gorge where Pre-Cambrian rock piles up to ten thousand feet on either side. A raven creaks overhead, flies into the cleft, glides toward a panel of white water splashing over a ledge, and comes out cawing.

To find what is lost is an art in some cultures. The Navajos employ "hand tremblers," usually women, who go into a trance and "see" where the lost article or person is located. When I asked one such diviner what it was like when she was in trance, she said, "Lots of noise, but noise that's hard to hear."

Near the falls the ground flattens into a high-altitude valley before the mountains rise vertically. The falls roar, but they're overgrown with spruce, pine, willow, and wild rose, and the closer I get, the harder it is to see the water. Perhaps that is how it will be in my search for the dog.

We're worried about Frenchy because last summer he was bitten three times by rattlesnakes. After the first bite he walked toward me, reeled dramatically, and collapsed. I could see the two holes in his nose where the fangs went in, and I felt sure he was dying. I drove him twenty miles to the vet; by the time we arrived, Frenchy resembled a monster. His nose and neck had swollen as though a football had been sewn under the skin.

I walk and walk. Past the falls, through a pass, toward a larger, rowdier creek. The sky goes black. In the distance snow on the Owl Creek Mountains glares. A blue ocean seems to stretch between, and the black sky hangs over like a frown. A string of cottonwoods whose new, tender leaves are the color of limes pulls me downstream. I come into the meadow with the abandoned apple orchard. The trees have leaves but have lost most of their blossoms. I feel as if I had caught strangers undressed.

The sun comes back, and the wind. It brings no dog, but ducks slide overhead. An Eskimo from Barrow, Alaska, told me the reason spring has such fierce winds is so birds coming north will have something to fly on.

To find what's lost; to lose what's found. Several times I've thought I might be "losing my mind." Of course, minds aren't literally misplaced – on the contrary, we live too much under them. As with viewing the falls, we can lose sight of what is too close. It is between the distant and close-up views that the struggle between impulse and reason, logic and passion takes place.

The feet move; the mind wanders. In his journals Thoreau wrote: "The saunterer, in the good sense, is no more vagrant than the meandering river, which is all the while sedulously seeking the shortest course to the sea."

Today I'm filled with longings – for what I'm not, for what is impossible, for people I love who can't be in my life. Passions of all sorts struggle soundlessly, or else, like the falls, they are all noise but can't be seen. My hybrid anguish spends itself as recklessly and purposefully as water.

Now I'm following a game trail up a sidehill. It's a mosaic of tracks – elk, deer, rabbit, and bird. If city dwellers could leave imprints in cement, it would look this way: tracks would overlap, go backward and forward like the peregrine saunterings of the mind.

I see a dog's track, or is it a coyote's? I get down on my hands and knees to sniff out a scent. What am I doing? I entertain expectations of myself as preposterous as when I landed in Tokyo – I felt so at home there that I thought I would break into fluent Japanese. Now I sniff the ground and smell only dirt. If I spent ten years sniffing, would I learn scents?

The tracks veer off the trail and disappear. Descending into a dry wash whose elegant, tortured junipers and tumbled boulders resemble a Japanese garden, I trip on a sagebrush root. I look. Deep in the center of the plant there is a bird's nest, but instead of eggs, a locust stares up at me.

Some days I think this one place isn't enough. That's when nothing is enough, when I want to live multiple lives and be

allowed to love without limits. Those days, like today, I walk
with a purpose but no destination. Only then do I see, at least
momentarily, that everything is here. To my left a towering cottonwood is lunatic with birdsong. Under it I'm a listening post
while its great gray trunk – like a baton or the source of something – heaves its green symphony into the air.

　　I walk and walk: from the falls, over Grouse Hill, to the dry
wash. Today it is enough to make a shadow.

SUZANNAH LESSARD

FROM

The Talk of the Town

THE BELLS of Trinity Church struck noon under a dark-gray sky as I emerged from the subway at Wall Street. The winter that has passed now was just beginning. On the street in front of the church, a trio played jungly music that got mixed up with the church bells. I followed a narrow, lumpy street into the depths of the financial district, where I found the hugely brass-knobbed door of a venerable masculine lunch club. Inside, its character was plain, but with subtle flavors underneath – like a stew cooked over a low flame for a long time. An elderly figure in black tie spotted me, lurched, then sprinted toward me. "You want Room E-F," he said, and he repeated "Room E-F," emphatically, meaning *"Do not stray."* I didn't. Room E-F was warmly lit, not large, with tables arranged in a U and set for lunch. Natives of Wall Street were in the majority. I have noticed about members of the financial community gathered together in rooms in Manhattan that sometimes they look ghastly, almost as if they were dead, and sometimes they look like Rembrandts. The burghers in Room E-F that day had lively eyes and good color, and emanated evolved worldliness. Artistic persons and a variety of female persons, including some who had not camouflaged themselves as natives, were present as well. There was an atmosphere of openness and civility. Conversations wove naturally in and out of each other. This was pleasant, and completely unexpected. It was only a public-relations event.

A man was there whose eminence was based on a lifelong, and continuing, productivity of incontrovertible worth; he appeared to have the sort of harmonious nature for which work is almost like breathing. His eminence seemed to have risen up underneath him until it became a cliff top, on which he dwelt, cordial, alert, and unrivalrous. He seemed to know about but be strangely protected from the emergencies of the world – on some of which he was an expert – and from the subjective emergencies that toss the rest of us about, at the foot of the cliff. This man had unusually large eyes, which were blue – a dark, hot, tropical blue that was surprising. His eyes could seem to frame him, as if they were the sky behind him, as he leaned down from his cliff top to speak or listen – or, to put it the other way around, speaking to him, one had the impression of looking skyward. That day, in the course of conversation, this man spoke to me of a writer who, though eminent, had found no cliff top – had instead been, to the end of his days, battered by his own conflicted nature. The man on the cliff top spoke of a book, recently published, that exposes the tortured side of this writer's life in detail. It seemed almost inconceivable that the man on the cliff top had ever suffered in that way. He and the writer could easily be seen as opposites. But the man on the cliff top said that he had come away from the book loving the writer very much. He said this with candid simplicity. His saying this from his cliff top gave the impression that pain and confusion are not wasted but are also not paramount. His use of the word "love" was unembarrassed. For a moment, it was as if this man and the writer he spoke of were parts of the same nature; for a moment, the dark, hot blue that framed him seemed not empyrean at all but the inside of the sphere of consciousness which contains all of us, and within which we are allies against isolation, futility, and death. The hospitality of the room deepened. I looked out the window and saw snow falling. Time drew in thick and close, like a nurturing cocoon.

It's amazing to hear the word "love" used with a full-bodied meaning intact, and it was doubly amazing that day, for the meaning was unusual: love felt upon reading about a fellow-man, now dead, who had suffered. It was triply amazing to hear it used in a social situation: "love" is a word that, if we want to use it with its meaning intact, we reserve for moments that are quiet and intimate, so that its meaning won't be dissipated by a tumble of other meanings. But here, though it had been thrown out in the course of random conversation, its meaning remained intact and powerful, and, furthermore, it had seemed at home in the room; and why it should have seemed at home I couldn't say, because the people there were strangers gathered for a public-relations event. It was a spectacular little miracle.

Then a shift took place which reversed the miracle with a horrible authority. It was caused by a small thing: the manner of a waiter when I asked where a phone was – the controlling way he stood at the door to see that I went to the right place, and did not stray. It brought home the archaic exclusivity of the club, not only socially but in terms of male/female. It made me uncomfortable, and when I came back to the room it seemed to me that the civilized sociability was little more than a phantom borrowed from another century's habit of institutionalizing the abyss between men and women. But the authority behind the shift came from modern life, from the actuality of my firsthand experience. It came from my experience of what seems to be a perverse law of modern life: that the deeper the connection the more inevitable its breaking, and that the relationships between men and women must be a special target of this law. And it seemed to me that this target is not so much our relationships as lovers, where we can meet as opposites and from opposite ends of the earth, as our relationships as brothers and sisters, our relationships based on our sameness, our relationships as allies against the darkness in our common nature, against isolation, futility, and death. This law seemed to me to be Havoc itself in action. And a way to describe this invisible yet omnipresent abyss might be this: If a man says, "I came away from the book loving him very much," we all know he means as a brother. But if a man said of a book about a woman, "I came away from the book loving her very much," we would suspect that he meant he had, in some way, fallen *in* love with her, becauase the idea that he loved her as a sister would seem far-fetched. It would mean that he had admitted her experience into his own, and the word "love" does not currently delineate a sphere of experience within which men and women are part of the same nature, and allies. A man who used the word that way would be an extraordinary man. In this, somehow, we are not together. I thought: How can we reknit the world under these circumstances? That the warmth in the room evaporated was hardly remarkable – this was only a public-relations event. But it is always sad to look again and see that it's no longer snowing.

I stood on the street once more, opposite Trinity Church. Wall Street's church is very black – the absorbent black of night. It seems to be sucking all the light out of the air. It looks like a witch crouched among the skyscrapers – a witch with a pointy hat. It looks as if it were about to spring. From here, Broadway extends straight uptown to Eleventh Street. At Eleventh Street, it bends like an elbow, and in the crook stands Grace Church. Grace Church is a frosty gray that gives off light. It looks like an angel, wings barely folded. It looks as if it had alighted on the earth just a moment before. Grace and Trinity Churches mark off an axis in the city. One can see them as jewels of tradition, fastening the ravelling, wind-snapped fabric of contemporary New York to the schist. Or one can see them as having become a kind of costume jewelry, worn by the city as by an irreverent, humorous girl. To me that day, they were masculine. To me that day, they were also clues, strewn along the historical way – apparitions, both slightly eerie, of the light and the dark in our nature. The snow had stopped falling. In this, the day seemed stingy, and the season choked up, incapable of a full statement. And then the third shift of the day took place. It was as if the little miracle of before came back, took up residence inside me, and spoke. It said: Snow is not something that it makes sense to wait for or hope for, much less count on. But snow always comes eventually, and sometimes soon. And almost in spite of myself I thought: We will stand in rooms that are lamplit at midday and we will talk with an open civility that is not at odds with private experience. As we talk, it will begin to snow, and the mood in the room will change to a richer key. The snow will fall thickly, and then more thickly, until there is no doubt about the fullness of its arrival. The reciprocal hospitality in the room will deepen further, and time will gather in close around us, like a cocoon. I saw myself afterward, alone, on the street, in the snowfall. The snowflakes would land on my cheeks with the lightest touch on earth, then turn to tears, unaccompanied by sorrow – cool tears that would remind me of another time.

JAMES FENTON

✖

The Snap Election

The Project is Thwarted

A MAN SETS light to himself, promising his followers that he will rise again in three hours. When the time has elapsed, the police clear away the remains. Another man, a half-caste, has himself crucified every year – he has made a vow to do this until God puts him in touch with his American father. A third unfortunate, who has lost his mother, stands rigid at the gate of his house and has been there, the paper tells us, for the last fourteen years, "gazing into an empty rubber plantation."

I don't know when it was that I began noticing stories like these, or began to think that the Philippines must be a strange and fascinating place. Pirates came from there last year to attack a city in Borneo. Ships sank with catastrophic loss of lives. People came from all over the world to have psycho-surgeons rummage through their guts – their wounds opened and closed in a trice. There was a Holy War in Mindanao. There was a communist insurgency. Political dialogue was conducted by murderers. Manila was a brothel.

It was the Cuba of the future. It was going the way of Iran. It was another Nicaragua, another Cambodia, another Vietnam. But all these places, awesome in their histories, are so different from each other that one couldn't help thinking: this kind of talk was a shorthand for a confusion. All that was being said was that something was happening in the Philippines. Or more plausibly: a lot of different things were happening in the Philippines. And a lot of people were feeling obliged to speak out about it.

But still at this stage, although the tantalizing little items were appearing daily in the English press, I had not seen any very ambitious account of what was going on. This fact pleased me. I thought that if I planned well in advance, engineered a decent holiday and went off to Manila, I would have the place to myself, as it were. I would have leisure and space enough to work away at my own pace, not running after a story, not hunting with the pack of journalists. I would watch, and wait, and observe. I would control my project rather than have it control me.

But I had reckoned without the Reagan administration and the whims of a dictator. Washington began sending urgent and rather public envoys to Manila, calling for reforms and declaring that time was running out. There was something suspicious in all this. It looked as if they were trying to fix a deal with Marcos — for if they weren't trying to fix things the alternative view must be that they were destabilizing the dictatorship, and this seemed out of character. Then Marcos went on American television and announced a snap election. And this too smelled fishy. I couldn't imagine that he would have made such a move had he not been certain of the outcome. For a while it was uncertain whether the snap election could or would be held, for the terms which the dictator offered to his people appeared unconstitutional. The constitution required that Marcos resign before running again for office. But Marcos would not resign: he would offer a post-dated resignation letter only, and he would fight the presidential election in his role as president.

In other words, the deal was: Marcos would remain president but would hold a fair election to reassure his American critics that he still had the support of his people; if, by some fluke, it turned out that he did not have this support, the world had his word of honour that he would step down and let somebody else be president. And this somebody else, in all probability, would be the woman who was accusing Marcos of having murdered her husband. So if he stepped down, Marcos would very likely be tried for murder.

It didn't sound as if it was going to be much of an election.

What's more, it was going to wreck my dream of having Manila all to myself. Indeed, my project was already in ruins. By now everybody in the world seemed to have noticed what an interesting place the Philippines was. There would be a massive press corps running after every politician and diplomat. There would be a deluge of background articles in the press. People would start getting sick of the subject well before I had had the chance to put pen to paper.

I toyed with the idea of ignoring the election altogether. It was a sham and a fake. It would be a "breaking story." If I stuck to my original plan, I would wait till Easter, which is when they normally hold the crucifixions. I wasn't going to be panicked into joining the herd.

Then I panicked and changed all my plans. Contrary to some expectations, the opposition had united behind Corazón Aquino, the widow of the national hero Benigno "Ninoy" Aquino. She was supposedly an unwilling candidate, and supposedly a completely inexperienced politician. But she was immensely popular – unwillingness and inexperience, it appeared, made a refreshing change. The assassination of her husband in 1983, as he stepped off the plane in Manila airport, was a matter that had never been cleared up. So there was a highly personal, as well as political, clash ahead.

(Not everybody believes, I was to discover, that President Marcos personally authorized the murder. At the time, one is assured, he was having one of his relapses. A man who was involved in the design of the presidential dentures told me, meaningly, that at the time of Ninoy's death Marcos's gums were very swollen – which was always a sign. And he added, intriguingly, that whenever Marcos's gums were swollen, the gums of General Ver, the Chief of Staff, swelled up in sympathy. Marcos was in the military hospital at the time, and I have it from someone who knew one of his nurses that, when

he heard the news, Marcos threw his food-tray at his wife,
Imelda. Others say he slapped her, but I prefer the food-tray
version.)

In addition to the growing opposition to Marcos in the Philippines, there was the discrediting campaign in the United
States, which began to come up with some interesting facts and
theories. Marcos's vaunted war record had been faked. His
medals were fakes. His property holdings overseas were vast.
He was shifting huge sums of dollars back to the Philippines to
finance the coming campaign. He was seriously ill from lupus
erythematosus. He had had two kidney transplants, but whether
he still had two kidneys was another matter. His supporters
painted slogans around Manila:

WE ♡ FM

His opponents, many of whom had a rough sense of humour,
changed these to

LUPUS ♡ FM

At the outset of the campaign he was obviously very ill. One
day his hands were mysteriously bleeding. Had he received the
stigmata? He was carried into meetings on a chair. Perhaps he
would be dead before the campaign was through.

Foreign observers had been invited to see fair play in the elections. There was Senator Lugar and his American team, and
there was an international team. Around a thousand journalists arrived, plus other freelance observers. So that when I
boarded my plane at Gatwick on 30 January, it was with a sense
of being stampeded into a story. I had no great hope of the
elections. I was going just in case.

A Loyal Marcos Man

THERE'S A SPECIAL kind of vigilance in the foyer of a press
hotel. The star TV correspondents move through, as film stars
do, as if waiting to be recognized, spotted. When they come
back sweating and covered with the dust of the road, they have

a particular look which says: See I have come back sweating, covered with the dust of the road. When they leave in a hurry on a hot news tip, they have a look which says: What? Me leave in a hurry on a hot news tip? No, I'm just sloping off to dinner. Everyone is alert to any sudden activity – the arrival of a quotable politician, the sudden disappearance of a rival crew, the hearty greetings of the old hands. When the foyer is full, it is like a stock exchange for news. When it is empty, you think: Where *are* they all? What's going on?

I was frisked at the door of the Manila Hotel. It was government-owned, and nobody was taking any chances. The bellboys came past wheeling massive displays of flowers. In the brown air beneath the chandeliers, obvious agents were keeping a track of events. The hotel telephone system was working to capacity, and there was trouble with crossed lines. But I finally got through to Helen, my main contact in Manila, and we agreed to meet in the Taproom.

Here the atmosphere was green from the glass reading-lamps on the bar. A pale, shrunken face was knocking back some strong mixture. Hearing me order, the face approached me and made itself unavoidable. "You're English, aren't you? You see? I can always tell. What you doing?"

"I'm a tourist."

That made him laugh. "Tourist? I bet you're M. I. Sixteen." I thought, if he wants me to be M. I. Sixteen, that's fine by me. I stared into my whisky as if to confirm his analysis. By now he was rather close. I wondered how long it would take Helen to "wash up and finish a few things." My companion ordered another Brandy Alexander. He was going to get very drunk that night, he said, then he would get him a girlfriend.

He was English like me, he said, only he had been deported at the age of eight. Now his Filipina wife had left him, and at midnight it would be his birthday. Could he see my matches? Those were English matches, weren't they? I passed him the box. He was, he said, the only white man to have worn the uniform of Marcos's bodyguard.

Or maybe he said palace guard. He was wearing a *barong tag-alog*, the Filipino shirt that you don't tuck in. He'd been at the palace that day – he'd just come from there – and he'd been in big trouble. Hadn't had the right clothes. Just look, he said, there are darns in my trousers. His wife had left him and she had taken all his clothes – everything. Now he was going to get drunk, get him a girl and go home at midnight.

Since it was my turn to talk, I suggested that he find the girl first, then go home.

"It's my *birthday*," he said, staring at his watch under the reading-lamp to see how long he had to drink till midnight. He had five hours in hand. His car was parked outside. I suggested he take a taxi home. He told me he had the biggest police car in Manila. I suggested he get a policeman to drive him home. He ordered another Brandy Alexander. The waiters smiled nervously at him and called him Colonel. I began to think he might be for real.

He lurched forward confidentially. "I'm a loyal Marcos man," he said, but this election…" He shook his head. "He'll win it," he said, "but it'll be a damn close thing. He'll lose in Metro Manila. Marcos is a great man, but it's the people around him. There's so much corruption at the palace. So many corrupt people…"

I didn't want any more of his confidences. I'd been here a couple of hours, and I wasn't going to be drawn. I said: "Tell me about your ring." It was as big as a stud-box.

"Oh," he said, "it started off as a piece of jade, then I had my initials put on it, then the setting" – it seemed to include diamonds – "and then the stone fell out and I stuck it back with superglue."

I thought it must be superglue, I said. In addition to the ring he had a heavy gold watch and an identity bracelet, all gross and sparkling.

"The Queen gave me a medal," he said. "And my wife threw it in the trash-can! She threw it away! Look, she tied a knot in the ribbon!"

He fished the medal out of his trouser pocket. "That's a George III medal," he said. "I'm English and proud of it. Any time I want, I can go back to Cheshire and eat kippers."

Then he said, "Would you do me a favour?"

I panicked a little.

"Those matches," he said, "English matches. Would you give them to me? You see, if I show these at the Palace, everyone'll be surprised. They won't know where I got them from. We don't have them here."

I gave him the matches. "What are you doing this evening?" he asked.

"I'm afraid I have a dinner appointment."

He laughed at these little panics he knew how to create, and told me not to worry. He wasn't going to barge in on my night out. We returned to the subject of his wife. He produced a letter and told me to read it out loud.

It was very dark in the bar, so we had to huddle together by the reading light. The letter was from the Minister of Tourism: "Dear _____," I read, "Please remember that _____ is your husband and the father of your two children. Please give him back his clothes so that he can recover his self-respect.

"Read it out," said the colonel, "read it out loud."

Then he told me that Marcos could do nothing to help him. His wife had taken everything, the children, his clothes, the lot. The case was in a civil court and Marcos could do nothing about it.

This was the first time I had heard of a court beyond Marcos's control. I could see what the colonel meant about going back to Cheshire and eating kippers.

Pedro's Party

WHEN HELEN arrived the colonel looked startled and impressed. I was impressed too. I hadn't expected Helen to look like Meryl Streep. The colonel shot me a look and I shot one back. He wanted to tell Helen about his wife. "I'm sorry," I said, "but we're late for our meeting." Then I took the surprised Helen and propelled her across the floor.

"What's going on?" she said. I was just afraid we might be landed with him all evening.

It turned out, though, that there *was* a meeting in hand. That is, one of Helen's friends, Pedro, was giving a party, and if I wanted to go, if I could stay awake after dinner, I was welcome. Pedro's family were squatters, and I noticed – without realizing how customary this was in the Philippines – that at the end of the meal Helen and I had together, she packed up the remains of our food and took it with us for Pedro's children.

I was impressed by Helen: she seemed to know everyone on the street, and most of them by name. People greeted her from the café as we passed, and the cigarette vendors called out to us. We turned down a little alley-way and into a garden beneath a mango tree. Pedro's hut consisted of a single room with a covered extension. There was a large fridge outside, painted green, with a "Bad Bananas" sticker, and posters advertising a performance of *Antigone* and a concert by an American pianist. Helen disappeared indoors to talk to the women and children, while the rest of us drank beer around a table. There were reporters, photographers and theatre people, and members of the foreign press corps, also friends of Helen. I was beginning to get the idea. We were all friends of Helen. She had a whole society of friends.

The great conversation topic was what had just happened in the Manila Hotel. There had been a press conference. As Marcos had been brought in, the *Paris Match* photographer had held his camera in the air to get a shot of him. Two of Marcos's bodyguards had tried to snatch the camera, and the photographer had tried to elbow them away. He had been hustled out of the room and into the hotel kitchen, where the bodyguards had taken turns beating him up. The chef who had been passing was knocked over in the mêlée, and dropped the special cake he had prepared in Marcos's honour.

The party grew, and grew noisy. People taught me the political signs. The Laban sign was an L made with the thumb and first finger. That was the sign for Cory's campaign – "Laban" was Tagalog for "fight." The sign for the KBL, Marcos's party, was a V. If you turned your hand over and rubbed your thumb and fourth finger together, that was the sign for money, the bribe, the greasing of the machine. The boycott sign was an X, two fingers crossed, or two clenched fists across your chest. Many of the people present were solidly, and others liquidly, behind the election boycott. "We're all partisans here!" shouted one guy. He was wearing a red baseball cap with a red star, and an embroidered badge saying "Don't shoot journalists." No joke, that. Of the thirty journalists killed worldwide last year, half had been Filipinos. Several of the company were wearing the *tubao*, a purple and yellow kerchief which showed, if you wore it, you had probably been to "the hell of Mindanao," one of the worst areas of the war.

Pedro moved among the guests, and plundered the crates of San Miguel beer. People tied their kerchiefs over their noses and made fearsome gestures, laughing hugely. A guitar was passed around and songs were sung from the war of independence against the Spanish. Helen sang too. She seemed to improvise a song in Tagalog, and this was doubly surprising because she had been complaining of laryngitis earlier in the evening. Now her voice had woken up for the occasion. It was deep and throaty. She was singing about the Mendiola Bridge, where all the big demonstrations ended up, and where the army or the police used to disperse the crowd with water-cannon and tear gas.

There was another song about the Mendiola Bridge which went simply:

> Mendiola Bridge is falling down
> Falling down
> Falling down
> Mendiola Bridge is falling down
> My First Lady.

The First Lady being Imelda Marcos. I had heard she was very superstitious, always off to the soothsayer. One day she was told the three things that would happen before the Marcos regime fell: a major earthquake would destroy a church; a piece of earth would erupt after a long silence; and the opposition would cross Mendiola Bridge by force. Since that prophecy had been made, Marcos had spent 2.4 million dollars restoring a church in his native Ilocos Norte for his daughter Irene's wedding. A few weeks after the ceremony there had been an earthquake and the fault had run right through the church. Then the Mayon volcano had erupted after a long silence. As for the third condition, some people said it had already been fulfilled when some opposition people had been allowed across the bridge. But others said no: it must be crossed by force. The bridge was the point of defence along the road to the Malacañang Palace. I imagined that, to have achieved such a significance, it must be a great big handsome bridge. I certainly did not think that I should see the crowds swarm over it. But I was wrong on both counts.

The Americans at the party obviously shared Helen's love for the Filipinos, although they had not been here as long as she had. While I sat there blearily congratulating myself on having arrived and actually *met* people, they were thick in an involvement which I was yet to feel. I could see that they were really delighted to be at Pedro's house, a piece of somewhat haphazard carpentry. I too felt honoured. But I sensed in the Americans a feeling of guilt about the Filipinos, and when I asked one of them what was happening he said: "It's all a sordid and disgusting deal. Marcos has everything on his side – the army, the police, the banking system, the whole apparatus. He's going to fix the election, and Washington is going to go along with it."

Then he gave me a sharp look and said: "You know what you're suffering from. You're suffering from jet-lag denial." It was quite true. Pedro found me a taxi to the hotel.

My hotel, the Philippines Plaza, was a big mistake, perhaps

my biggest mistake so far. When people heard I was staying there, they couldn't believe my bad judgment. The thing I couldn't explain to any of them was that I had needed the name of a hotel in order to tell the NPA where they could contact me. By coincidence, a friend from Ethiopia had been staying at this place and had dropped me a note. So now I was stuck in this isolated monstrosity, which I had known only by name, in the vain hope that I would receive some message. In order to deliver the message, the NPA would have to get past the matador on the front door. From what I knew of the NPA, that would be no problem. But what about me? I was a bad case of jet-lag denial. The matador, both of him, saluted and opened the taxi door. I paid my fare and stumbled out, at the height of his frogged breeches.

Among the Boycotters

HARRY AND JOJO picked me up the next morning. I felt fine, really fine. They, less so. Pedro's party had taken it out of them. Harry asked what I had expected of Manila. I paused. "Probably from abroad you think there are killings going on all the time," said Harry, "but you know…they do the killings mostly at night." And he laughed a good deal.

"Why are you laughing, Harry?" I said. "I don't think that's funny at all."

"You don't think it's funny. Europeans never think it's funny if someone's killed. But you know, we Filipinos, sometimes there are demonstrations where two or three people are killed, and immediately afterwards people are joking and fooling around. You have to joke in order to keep going. But I've noticed Europeans never joke about these things."

He had been to Europe on business. Photography was only a sideline for him. He wanted me to know that the people we were about to see this morning, the Bayan marchers, were the most important people in the election. "At the end," said Harry, "once the Cory supporters see that it has all been a fix, many of them will join Bayan, or return to its ranks." The marches would go on, up and down the country. That was the important thing, and he insisted on the point throughout the day. Sometimes I would look at Harry and think: He's as proud of Bayan as if they were his sons and daughters, as if he were living through their achievements. At other times I felt I was being pressed for a response, a confidence. I couldn't reconcile my idea of Harry the owner of the small export business with Harry the admirer of the Left.

Bayan, the umbrella organization for the legal, "cause-oriented" groups in the opposition, was said by some to be nothing but a communist front. Others emphasized the diversity of political opinion within its ranks. I asked many people in subsequent weeks what the truth of the matter was. A Communist told me: "It's not a communist front – it *is* the Communists." Others strongly rejected this. A Bayan member told me: "It's like this. When the Communists speak, we listen to what they say. When Bayan speaks, they listen to us. We are neighbours. I never see my neighbour from one week to the next, but when he is cooking, I know what he'll be having for dinner." It was an open secret, he said, that within four years the NPA would be marching through Manila. When that happened, Bayan would have helped them.

Harry said: "Maybe there'll be some trouble today as the marchers come into the city. Maybe we'll see something."

I said: "I very much hope not." I enjoyed disconcerting Harry with a resolutely anti-good-story line.

Harry said: "You know, photographers – they love it when trouble begins.

I wasn't looking for trouble.

We drove south on the highway, past small businesses, authorized dealers in this and that, scrappy banana palms, pawnshops, factories – some with their own housing estates adjacent – American-style eateries, posh condominiums and slums. As a first impression it offered nothing very shocking.

Just beyond Muntinlupa we met the marchers, about a thousand of them with banners denouncing the U.S.-Marcos dictatorship. Most of them were masked. They looked young, and I would have thought that they were students, but Harry insisted they were mainly peasants and workers. I was asked to sign a piece of paper explaining who I was. Most journalists, I realized, wore plasticated ID tags round their necks. In the absence of this, you were assumed to be from the American Embassy. A masked figure passed me with a megaphone, and shouted: "Down with U.S. imperialism."

"They're very well organized," said Harry. "You'll see. They're ready for anything." And it was true – they had their own first aid team and an ambulance. They quite expected to be shot. If Bayan was the legal arm of the people's struggle it was still organized like an army. The march was divided into units, and when they stopped at the Church of Our Lady you could see how the units stayed close together to avoid infiltration. As the march approached Manila they were expecting trouble from goons. It was clear that they were very experienced marchers and knew exactly how to maintain control of their numbers.

The people at the church had not made them welcome, but they took over the building nevertheless. Rice and vegetables were brought from the market, and they ate in groups, or rested in the cool of the building, under the crucified figure of the Black Nazarene, whose wavy brown wig reached down to his waist.

The marchers had seemed hostile at first, and I was in no hurry to talk to them if they didn't want to talk to me. Finally I met Chichoy, who was I suppose in his early twenties, and whose political work, he told me, was in educating peasants and workers towards a state of mind where they did not consider their grievances to be part of an inevitable order of things. It was good work and had produced gratifying results. But, as Chichoy said at one point, "People like me do not live long. We are prepared to die at any time. The point is not to have a long life – a long life would be a good thing – the point is to have a

meaningful life." His way of speaking combined a serious firm-
ness of tone with a deep sadness, as if his own death in the cause
were something that he had often contemplated, very much
regretted, but there it was.

Not all of the Bayan marchers struck me like this. Some of
them seemed to relish the figures they cut, with their red flags
and facemasks, and their way of bringing drama onto the streets
in the manner of the Peking ballet. Chichoy talked about how
a fair election was an impossibility. He was adamant that the intention of the U.S. was to support a dictatorship either way — if
not Marcos, an alternative Marcos. If Ninoy Aquino had not
been killed, maybe he would have become the alternative dictator. Firmly in his mind was the equation of the U.S. with dictatorship. The Americans had to be overthrown. Their bases
had to be closed down. The Philippines would become non-
aligned, "and that will be our contribution to world peace."

The march moved off. It was one of a series converging on
the city, and it joined with another group under the highway
at Muntinlupa. People shouted: "The Snap Election is a fake.
So what. We're going to the mountains." There were few police in sight, and nobody tried to stop the teams of girls with
paint pots, who scrawled hurried slogans on the kerbs and
walls. On a house which was decked with Marcos posters, I noticed a window full of boycott placards being waved wildly by
unseen people. Bayan had its supporters — over a million of
them in the country, it was said. But the crowds did not join in.
It was as if these demonstrators were on a dangerous mission
of their own. The people watched them and kept their own
counsel.

We were marching underneath the raised highway, and the
acoustics were tempting. When the firecrackers started exploding, the demonstrators cheered. For my part, I became extremely anxious. We had been expecting trouble, and I couldn't tell
whether it was the demonstrators who were lobbing the firecrackers or the crowd. I didn't yet know that this was part of the
Bayan style. I asked Harry, "Who's throwing those things?"

"I don't know," he said, clicking away. He hadn't caught the sense of my question.

The Bayan style was to make each demonstration look and sound as dangerous as possible. When the marches converged on Manila that evening, and the demonstrators sealed off roads by linking arms, the speed and drama with which they operated made it look as if a revolution was in the offing. The defiance of the slogans, the glamour of the torches, the burning tyres, the masked faces – it was a spectacular show. But the State was adopting an official policy of Maximum Tolerance, and the demonstrators had the streets to themselves.

The next day they came together and marched towards Malacañang. And so we arrived at the famed Mendiola Bridge, where the barricades were up, a massive press corps stood in waiting, and the military blocked the way. The bridge was insignificant enough: you wouldn't have noticed it if you had not been looking for it. On the side streets, U.S. Embassy men with walkie-talkies were giving up-to-date accounts of the action. "You ought to have a mask," said Helen, "there may be a dispersal." But the tear gas was not used, and the water-cannon was only there for display. They burned effigies of Reagan and Marcos at the front of the barricade. Reagan caught alight easily, but Marcos was slow to burn.

Overheard

The telephones in the Manila Hotel were somewhat overloaded. Here is a conversation Helen overheard on a crossed line on Sunday, 2 February.

> voice one: This is the problem, *compadre*. We're planning to go to Central Luzon and Tarlac on Monday. I'm sure you understand my position as the chairman. I can't just support the campaign for Marcos by words alone. I need the paper.

VOICE TWO: Yes, yes. Go ahead.

VOICE ONE: We need at least 10,000 pesos deposited by Monday to take care of the people there.

VOICE TWO: Well, I'll see what I can do.

VOICE ONE: If it's possible, I'd really like to pick up at least part of it this afternoon or early this evening. You know, if I could, I would just go to Malacañang to ask, but I don't want to go ask the President himself at this time. You know what I mean? Do you think it's possible?

VOICE TWO: OK, come on over.

VOICE ONE: I don't really want to call again. It's difficult on the phone. It's better if I see you. Oh, one more thing, Mr. _____, I've got some news. I've just come back from _____ and the word there is Marcos-Laurel.

VOICE TWO: Well, anyway, the important thing is that Macoy himself gets back in. If the VP needs to be sacrificed that doesn't matter. Right? *(They both laugh and say goodbye.)*

The Marcos-Laurel idea was much in the air at the time. Marcos's own vice-presidential candidate was Tolentino, but the theory was that if a close election was engineered in which Cory lost but her vice-president Doy Laurel won, the Americans might feel that honour had been satisfied. Marcos could say: You see? It is as I told you. The people would not vote for a woman president, let alone a completely inexperienced politician.

Rival Rallies

I NEVER FOUND out whether it was actually true, but people said in a very confident way that Marcos had seeded the clouds in the hope of producing a downpour for Cory's *miting de avance*. If he did, it was another of his miscalculations – like the calling of the Snap Election. The Laban supporters had asked for the grandstand in Luneta Park, just by the Manila Hotel. They weren't allowed it, and were obliged to put up their own platform facing the opposite way. The park filled up. The grandstand itself filled up. The meeting overflowed. People tried to guess how many there were in the crowd – a million, two million? It was impossible to tell. It was the biggest rally I'd ever been in, and one of the friendliest and funniest.

I sat among the crowd just in front of the platform. We were jammed so tight that sitting itself was very difficult. But if we stood we got shouted at by the people behind us, whereas if we shouted at the people in front of us to sit down they literally could not do so. It was very painful, and went on for seven or eight hours. What a relief when the dancing girls came on, or when we all stood for a performance of "Tie a Yellow Ribbon Round the Old Oak Tree," Ninoy's old campaign song. The idiom of the rally was distinctly American, with extra-flash gestures, like the priest on the platform who ripped open his soutane to reveal a yellow Cory T-shirt, or Butz Aquino in his Texan hat, or the yellow-ribboned pigeons and the fireworks overhead.

It was not easy for a newcomer to tell the difference between the pop-singers and professional crooners on the one hand, and the politicians and their wives and families on the other. Everyone sang – current hits, old favourites, I don't know what. The most electrifying speaker was undoubtedly Doy Laurel, although by the time he came on the anticipation was such that his work was easy. People had said Cory was not a professional politician. She was a professional something, though, taking the microphone and singing the Lord's Prayer. After the rabble-rousing of Laurel, the occasion had turned solemn and moving. When the crowd sang *"Bayan Ko,"* the national anthem of the Opposition, you felt all the accumulated laughter and cheering of the day turn into pure emotion. Religion and national feeling were at the heart of what Cory stood for.

THE NEXT DAY, Marcos had to do something about all this. The world's press had seen the great crowds. He had to come up with something equally impressive.

I sat on the balcony of my hotel room, with its view of Manila

Bay. Helicopters were passing to and fro across the city. Ships arrived, laden down with people. Army trucks and coaches were busing in the Marcos supporters, who formed up in groups in the hotel forecourt, in order to march down to Luneta.

Helen arrived with Jojo and Bing, another of her gang. They'd come down from Quezon City, where the streets were alive with anger. The Marcos supporters were being stoned as they arrived from the boondocks. We went back to have a look.

The taxi-man looked faintly nervous. He was carrying a Marcos flag – all the taxis at the Plaza did the same. He said: "I think we may be stoned."

I said: "Wouldn't it be a good idea to remove that flag?" As soon as we were out of sight of the hotel, he did.

Along the road the "noise barrage" had begun – long and short blasts on the horn, for *Co-ry*. Groups had gathered at street-corners to jeer the buses as they passed. From the car in front of us people were handing out Marcos T-shirts to the other drivers. When a busload of Marcos supporters came past, we found they were all leaning out of the windows making the Laban sign and calling for Cory. Helen asked them what they were up to. Oh, they said, we're all Cory supporters here – we're only doing it for the money. And they laughed at us: we were going to have to pay for our taxi, they said, whereas they were being paid to ride in their bus. They all treated the occasion as a tremendous joke. It was worth their while attending a Marcos rally for a couple of dollars. Such sums were not easy to come by.

Bing and I were walking towards the meeting. An enormous number of people in T-shirts were already walking away from it. Bing asked them, straight-faced, "Has Marcos spoken already?" No, they said. Then why were they leaving the meeting? They looked at him as if he were mad. They'd already had enough.

And now the clouds broke, and people really *had* had enough. As we ran for shelter in the Manila Hotel, the hired supporters (not one of whom would normally have been allowed to set foot in it) realized that they could hardly be turned away in their full Marcos paraphernalia. They stormed the foyer, pushing their way past the security guards and treating the whole occasion as a wonderful joke.

Marcos had been due to speak in the evening, but at this rate there wasn't going to be anybody left. So they brought him forward for an earlier rant.

And afterwards, no doubt, they called for the guy who had been told to seed the clouds, and gave him a very nasty time indeed.

Helen on Smoky Mountain

"WITHIN THAT American body," says Jojo, "there's a Filipino soul struggling to escape." Or another way of putting it was: "Helen is the first victim of Filipino imperialism." She has found herself in another language, and indeed she is in some danger of losing her American identity altogether. Among the circle of friends to whom she introduced me, she speaks English – when she speaks it – with a Filipino accent. Or perhaps it is more a matter of intonation. She will say: "There's going to be violence." She leans towards the end of the sentence. Instead of saying, "They were *shooting* at me," she says, "They were shooting at *me*." And she has forgotten the meaning of several English words.

English people sometimes find life relaxing in a foreign language if it means that they can lose their class backgrounds. Americans, rather lacking this incentive, don't seem to like to unbend linguistically. Whenever I meet really good American linguists, I always assume they're on a journey away from something. I don't ask Helen very much about her past. It's not that I'm not impertinent. I pride myself on being just as impertinent as the next man. But whenever I garner little details about her past, it's so dramatic that I don't know what to say. If I said, "So what does your little sister do now?" she would be bound to come up with something like, "She was eaten by a school of barracudas." And then I wouldn't know where to look.

She is essentially companionable and generous, and this leads her to do something I've never seen anybody do. She doesn't drink, but she enjoys the company of drinkers, and rather than lag behind as they get drunk, she gets mentally drunk first. One *calamansi* juice and she's slightly squiffy. After a couple of glasses of iced water she's well away.

Another unique feature: she's both a tomboy and a woman's woman. "What do you mean by a woman's woman?" she said one day, bridling. Well, what I meant was that she's the kind of woman women like. She goes into a house and within seconds, it seems, there are fascinating conversations taking place in the kitchen. Then suddenly all the women are going off to the cinema for a soppy movie in Tagalog. Helen has got them organized.

The tomboy side of Helen comes out in her professional life. The Filipino press corps is her gang, and she often says that it was a difficult gang to join, to be accepted by. There were suspicions. There were unkind rumours. She had to prove herself before she was considered one of the group. But by now the group in question is so large that going on a demonstration with Helen is like being taken to an enormous cocktail party which happens, for some reason, to be winding its way through the Manila streets toward the inevitable Mendiola Bridge. Hundreds and hundreds of introductions, slappings on the back, encounters with long-lost friends, wavings across a sea of heads.

Everything turns into a party around Helen. You suggest a working dinner *à deux*. By the evening in question it has turned into a feast *à huit*, with further complications about where to go afterwards, because another part of the party is waiting on the other side of the city, a third group is in the offing and there is even a chance that somebody she would like you to meet might turn up at a place which isn't exactly next door to where we are going but...

You have to consider this party as an event which is taking place all over Manila – like a demonstration.

One of the things that makes Helen really angry is the brothel aspect of Manila. The mere act of walking down certain Ermita streets is enough to send her into a passionate rage. She cannot relax among the sleaze – that would be a kind of connivance. If Helen's Filipino friends are rather curious to see the bars (which cater largely, it would appear, to Australians), she cannot follow them. Her rage would stand like a bouncer at the door, blocking her path.

She has a heroic conception of the Filipino people. The opposite conception – of an easy-going, lackadaisical, prostituted and eventually degraded nation – this she will fight against. You cannot help noticing that the struggle of the Filipino is carried on in the deepest recesses of her mind. Once she was saying, "Anyway, even if Cory Aquino were to become President of the United States of America, that wouldn't change anything – "

"Helen, do you realize what you've just said? Cory isn't standing for President of the United States of America."

"Is that what I said? Oh, so that's really Freudian, *huh*?"

"Yup." The Filipino struggle is the missing radical wing of American politics. This is Helen's discovery.

THE CAR STOPS at a red light and the pathetic moaning children beg for money.

"I'm not going to give money to you," says Helen to a boy. "You just give it to the police."

The boy is scandalized and drops the moaning immediately. "How do you know we give money to the police?"

"Everyone knows the police organize you kids. There's been gossip about it for years."

"Well if you spread gossip like that, that means *you're* a gossip," he snaps. Helen laughs. It's obvious that the gossip is true. The police take a cut from the street-urchins, just as they get money from the child prostitutes. Another Manila specialty.

Manila is a city of more than eight million, of whom three to four million live in the Tondo slums. And in some of these slums you see people who are barely managing to remain on the brink of existence. Smoky Mountain, one of the main garbage-dumps of Metro Manila, is such a place. The people live from scavenging plastic or polythene which is then sold to dealers and re-cycled. The mountain itself provides a living for rival communities who take it in turns to go out and sift the garbage. Sometimes there are quarrels over the shifts, and the scavengers actually fight over the tip. The worst work is by night: it is said that the truck-drivers pay no attention to the scavengers and drive over them.

Infant mortality among the scavengers is sixty-five to seventy per cent. The people live in huts at the foot of the tip, by the banks of the filthy Pasig River, a sewer in which they wash. It is here, by the bridge, that they sometimes find the mutilated victims of the latest "salvaging."

Coming here with Helen is like trailing in the wake of royalty. Word passes among the huts, the children swarm around her, they all know her by name, and she seems to know a great number of them. She loves making children laugh. She keeps a glove puppet in her camera bag for the purpose.

Up on the burning heap itself, I meet a boy who can say two sentences in English. "I am a scabenger, I am a scabenger," he repeats, and "This is garbage." He makes me feel the top of his head, which has a perfectly round dent three inches across, where he was beaten up, and he opens his shirt to show me a scar running from his neck to his navel, a war wound from one of the scavengers' battles. In his hand he holds a piece of cloth, like a comforter. He is high on solvent.

He tells Helen of his desperation and asks for her help, but she is severe with him. She says she'll only help him if he gives up the solvent. He says he only takes it because life is so desperate. She says she knows all about that. She's been a drug addict herself. But addiction doesn't help any.

Helen is hard on herself. In work, she likes to push herself to the limit. All the day it's go, go, go until the point when she's about to keel over. At that moment, all other expressions leave her face, and what you see is panic. When I catch her pushing herself to this point, I want to boss her about, like some Elder Brother from Outer Space.

But nobody bosses Helen about. She has her own destiny.

Election Eve: Davao

THERE IS a way of seeing without seeming to see. Harry had it to a certain degree. An eyebrow moves. A quiet word alerts your attention to the fact that something is going on. But it is no use expecting to be able to follow the direction of a gaze, in order to work out what you are supposed to be taking in. The seer will not give himself away. He is entirely surreptitious.

I noticed it first with Harry among the boycotters in Muntinlupa. We were sitting in the car not far from a peanut stall. What Harry was watching, without seeming to watch, was the behaviour of the policemen standing by the stall, keeping an eye on the Bayan rally. Casually, as they talked, they were helping themselves to the peanuts. The stall-holder made no protest. He was reading a comic. I suppose he too was seeing without seeming to see.

The policemen moved on. Then a plump figure in civilian clothes wandered past and the stall-holder passed him some notes. "What do you think he is?" I murmured to Harry.

"Looks like a gangster," he said. The man had been collecting the protection money. A small sum, no doubt, and it wasn't as if the policemen had been stuffing their faces with the peanuts. It was just that these were the kind of overheads a peanut vendor had to allow for.

Davao was quiet on election eve. It felt almost as if a curfew was in force. The sale of alcohol was prohibited, and there was no life around the market. Our driver had told us that there were salvagings almost every day — meaning that bodies were found and the people knew from the state of their mutilations that this was the work of the military. The driver had his own odd code. He told us that he wouldn't go along a certain street because there were a lot of dogs there and he couldn't stand dogs.

The eating-place we found was open to the street, and the positioning of its television meant that the clientele sat facing the outside world, but with their heads tilted upwards. There was a programme of Sumo wrestling, with a commentary in Japanese. Even the adverts were in Japanese. The clientele were drinking soft drinks. Nobody was talking. Everyone was watching the wrestling.

It seemed a hostile sort of place. We chose our food from the counter, but the waitress was slow and indifferent. Behind her on the wall was a Marcos sticker and, for good measure, a Cory sticker. I sat with my back to the street. Jojo and Helen were facing outwards.

At first I didn't notice that Jojo had seen something. Then I turned round and scrutinized the darkened street. Two jeeps had drawn up. I could see a man with a rifle disappearing into a house. Then a confusion of figures coming back to the vehicles, which drove swiftly off. In short, nothing much.

"They're picking someone up," said Jojo. "There'll probably be a lot of that tonight."

As far as I could tell, nobody else in the eating-place had observed the little incident. They were all engrossed in the wrestling. Except I didn't know how many of them had this gift of seeing without seeming to see.

Voting Day in Mindanao

It wasn't hard to tell which areas were going to vote for Marcos and which for Cory. In the Cory areas people were out on the road, cheering and waving and making the Laban sign. In the Marcos areas there was an atmosphere of quiet tension. The crowd, such as it was, did not speak freely. There was a spokesman who explained calmly and simply that Marcos had done so much for this village that there was no support for the opposition. As we could see, the explanation continued, there was no intimidation or harassment. People were voting according to their own free will. They all supported Marcos.

It was only out of earshot of this spokesman that members of my group were told *sotto voce* that they had been threatened with eviction if they voted the wrong way. Even so, some people said, they were not going to be coerced.

We drove to Tadeco, the huge banana plantation run by Antonio Florendo, one of the chief Marcos cronies. The Cory campaigners were hoping to get the votes from this area disqualified, as the register apparently featured far more names than Mr. Florendo employed. He had something like 6,000 workers, many of whom were prisoners. But the register had been wildly padded.

The polling station was at the centre of Mr. Florendo's domain. Rows and rows of trucks were lined up, and a vast crowd was milling around, waiting to vote. At the gates, a couple of disconsolate observers from NAMFREL, the National Movement for a Free Election, complained that they had been excluded from the station on the grounds that their papers lacked the requisite signatures. In fact the signatures were there and in order, but the people on the gate insisted this was not so. A sinister "journalist" began inquiring who I was, and writing down my particulars. "Oh, you come from England," he said menacingly. "Well, that may be useful if we all have to flee the country." Whenever I tried to speak to somebody, this man shoved his microphone under my nose.

We asked to speak to Mr. Florendo, and to our surprise he appeared, with an angry, wiry little lawyer at his side. The lawyer was trying to explain to us why the NAMFREL people should not be allowed in. He had a sheaf of papers to support his case. We introduced ourselves to Mr. Florendo, who looked like a character from *Dynasty* or *Dallas* – Texan hat, distinguished white hair, all smiles and public relations. He was a model employer. Everything here was above board. No, the register had not been padded – we could come in and see for ourselves. We asked him why the NAMFREL people had been excluded. He turned to his lawyer and said: "Is this so? Let them in, by all means." The lawyer expostulated and pointed to his sheaf of papers. Mr. Florendo waved him aside. Of course the NAMFREL people could come in. There was nothing to hide.

(One of the things they might have hidden better, which my companions noticed, was a group of voters lining up with ink on their fingers: they had already been through at least once.)

We asked if we could take Mr. Florendo's picture. "Oh," he said, "you must photograph my son, Tony-Boy – he's the handsome one." And he called to Tony-Boy, a languid and peculiarly hideous youth. Mr. Florendo thought that Tony-Boy could be a Hollywood star. I thought not. Mr. Florendo invited us to lunch. I thought not again. Mr. Florendo was overwhelming us with his honesty and generosity. He asked the crowd whether he was not a model employer, always available to his workers, and they all agreed that he was indeed a model employer.

In the early afternoon news came over the radio that the KBL had switched candidates, and that Imelda was now stepping in for her husband. "But they can't do that," I said. Oh yes they can, said the people in the car. For a while we believed the rumour. Jojo giggled helplessly. "If Imelda gets in, there really will be panic-buying. Only we've got no money to buy with. We'll just have to panic instead." And he flopped into a panic as he contemplated the awesome prospect.

Now the returns began to be announced over the NAMFREL radio. The idea was to do a quick count, so that the possibilities of tampering would be kept to a minimum. In precinct after precinct the results were showing Cory winning by a landslide. Around Davao alone they had expected her to get seventy per cent of the vote. And this indeed seemed possible. It all depended on what went on in the outlying areas such as Mr. Florendo's fief. NAMFREL could not observe everywhere. They simply didn't have enough people. But if they could monitor enough returns fast enough, they might be able to keep cheating to a minimum.

Davao, which features in stories as being one of the murder

capitals of the world, had had a quiet day. I think only two people had been killed. The NPA-dominated quarter called Agpao, and nicknamed Nicaragpao, had voted for Cory, although it was plastered with boycott posters, including one which showed the people taking to the mountains.

As the radio continued to announce Cory wins, Jojo came up with an idea. The votes could be converted into different currencies. Cory gets ten million votes, and these are expressed as rupees. Marcos gets five million, but these are dollars. So Marcos wins after all.

Certainly some kind of device was going to be needed.

In the hotel lobby, a desk had been set up to coordinate the results. The blackboard showed Cory with a healthy lead.

On the television, it appeared that far fewer of the results had so far been added up. Marcos was doing okay.

The figures in the lobby came from NAMFREL, which was the citizens' arm of the official tabulating organization, COMELEC. In the end it would be the COMELEC figures which counted. But the sources of both figures were the same certified returns. Something very odd was happening.

The head of NAMFREL was called Joe Concepción. The head of COMELEC was Jaime Opinión. The television told us to trust Mr. Opinión; the radio, Mr. Concepción.

Late that night, the COMELEC count ground to a complete halt. Something had gone wrong – and it was perfectly obvious what.

The NAMFREL Struggle

THERE WERE SEVERAL ways of fixing the election, all of which Marcos tried. The first was to strike names off the electoral register in areas of solid Cory support, and to pad out other registers with fictional names for the flying voters. You could bribe the voters with money and sacks of rice, or, aboveboard and publicly, with election promises. You could intimidate the solid areas. You could bribe the tellers. You could have fake ballot papers (a franking machine for these had gone missing for a whole week before the election). You could put carbon-paper under the ballot form, to make sure that an individual had voted the right way before you paid him off. You could print money for his pay-off, and if you printed the money with the same serial numbers there would be no record of how much you had printed. You could force the early closure of polling stations in hostile areas. You could do all these things and you might, if you were Marcos, get away with it.

But what if, after all that, the early returns made it plain that you still hadn't won?

Then you would have to start stealing the ballot boxes, faking the returns, losing the ballots, shaving off a bit here, padding a bit there and slowing down the returns so that, you hoped, once the initial wave of anger had subsided, you could eventually declare yourself the winner. To explain the delays in the counting of returns, there was a formula which never failed to unconvince. You could say over and over again on Channel Four, the government broadcasting station: "What the foreign observers fail to realize is that the Philippines is a nation comprised of over 7,000 islands. It takes a long time to collect the ballot boxes. Some of them have to be brought by boat or by carabao from very remote areas." But in the meantime votes would be taking a mysteriously long time to find their way from one side of Manila to the other.

This second phase of corruption was now beginning, and the people who stood against it were the NAMFREL volunteers and the Church. There was a great deal of overlap. Outside the town halls where the ballot boxes were kept and counted stood rows of nuns chanting Hail Marys, seminarians grouped under their processional crosses, Jesuits, priests and lay people. Outside Pasay Town Hall in Manila, the day after the election, I asked a Jesuit whether the whole of his order had taken to the streets in this way. He said that the only ones who hadn't were the foreigners, who didn't feel they could interfere. They were manning the telephones instead.

The Jesuit was a cheerful character. He told me that in the past members of his order used to go on retreat with Marcos once a year. He invited them down to a country residence of his in Bataan. They'd been very well catered to – food had come from a posh local restaurant. But Marcos himself had eaten very simply and kept retreat in the most pious manner. He had offered them the chance to go water-skiing, but the Coastguard had said there were too many jellyfish.

"What would the Pope have said," I asked him, "if you'd gone water-skiing? Would he have approved?"

"Maybe not," said the Jesuit. "Skiing yes, water-skiing perhaps no."

Anyway, these days of retreats with the Marcoses were now over. Not only were the Jesuits out on the streets. There were all kinds of people. At the same place I talked at length to a police cadet who was an ardent NAMFREL supporter. There were poor people and there were extremely elegant ladies – but elegant in the Cory, not the Imelda, style. In the trouble-spots, at Makati Town Hall and in the Tondo for instance, they had kept a vigil over the ballot boxes. They linked arms to protect them. They formed human chains to transport them. They all said, and they said it over and over again, that all they could do was protect the vote with their bodies. They were expecting harassment and they got it. They were expecting to be beaten up. They were expecting martyrdom and they got that too.

The expression, "the sanctity of the ballot," had been injected with real force, real meaning. It had been preached from every pulpit and it had sunk into every Catholic heart. The crony press was full of vituperation against the Church. It abominated Cardinal Sin. The Church that had once supported martial law, and had been courted by the Marcoses (Imelda was always swanning off to the Vatican), was now a public enemy. Paul's Epistle to the Romans was cited by the *Sunday Express* against the Church:

Everyone must obey state authorities, because no authority

> exists without God's permission, and the existing authorities
> have been put there by God. Whoever opposes the existing
> authority opposes what God has ordered; and anyone who
> does so will bring judgment on himself.

But they did not continue with the next verse: "For government, a terror to crime, has no terrors for good behaviour."
Which proves that Paul had not envisaged the Marcos dictatorship.

As THE NAMFREL struggle continued, and behind the scenes
the Marcos men were working out the best strategy for cooking
the books, Marcos himself gave a press conference at Malacañang. You couldn't get near the palace by taxi. You had to stop
at the beginning of a street called J. P. Laurel, then walk down
past some old and rather beautiful houses in the Spanish colonial style. As you came through the gate, you found that the
lawns had been turned over to the cultivation of vegetables in
little parterres. I wondered whether these were siege rations.
What were the Marcoses expecting? Beyond the vegetable garden lay a sculpture garden depicting mythological beings in
concrete. It looked rather as if some member of the family had
had a thing about being a sculptor, and been indulged in her
illusions.

A farther gate, a body search, and then you came to the
grand staircase flanked by carved wooden figures, leading up
to an anteroom where several grand ladies, Imelda-clones, sat
chatting. The room's decorations were heavy. There was an
arcaded gallery from which, I suppose, members of the Spanish
governor's household would have looked down on the waiting
petitioners. The anteroom led directly into a large and brightly
lit hall, got up very much like a throne room. Here the cameras
were all set up, and Marcos was in the process of explaining
that the delays of the night before had all been the fault of
NAMFREL. They had refused to cooperate with COMELEC in

what had been intended as a simultaneous and coordinated tabulation of results. However, that matter had all been cleared up earlier this morning. As far as the stopping of the count had been concerned, there had been no malicious, mischievous or illegal intent.

Marcos's eyes were lifeless. He could have been blind. Or perhaps he had only just been woken up. His mouth was an example of a thoroughly unattractive orifice.

He had his own set of figures, and he explained at great length how the arithmetic would work out. As he did so, his hand gestures were like those of a child imitating a plane taking off. He conceded he might have lost in Metro Manila. He conceded he had lost in Davao. But my moving his million-and-a-half votes from the Solid North all round the shop, so that you could never tell quite what he had set them off against, he managed to arrive at a "worst possible scenario" where he won by a million-and-a-half votes.

I couldn't follow him. Imelda had slipped in at the side and was watching in admiration. Like any bad actress she had a way of telling you: This is what's going through my mind, this is what I'm feeling. And the message she was putting across that day was: I've just slipped in, inconspicuously, to watch my husband brilliantly rebutting all the awful things that have been said about him by you foreign meddlers; look at him – isn't he wonderful? – *still*, at *his* age; how deeply I love him and how greatly I appreciate him; why is it that you lot can't see things the way I do? Don't look at me. I'm just sitting here admiring my husband, plain little inconspicuous me.

And she shook her head very gently from side to side, unable to believe how great he was, and how lucky she had been.

The COMELEC Girls at Baclaran

THE NEXT EVENING I was sitting with some Americans in the foyer of the Manila Hotel, wondering whether perhaps we might not have preferred to be in Haiti. There was after all something gripping about the way the people there had dug up Papa Doc's bones and danced on them. And what would happen to all the dictators in exile? *Rolling Stone* suggested a Dictator Theme Park, where we could all go to visit them in natural surroundings.

A chap came up to our table, hovering about three inches off the floor, his eyes dilated. He had taken some high-quality something. "Listen you guys, nobody move now because the opposition's watching. The COMELEC girls have walked out of the computer count, in protest at the cheating. The whole thing's fucked."

We got up casually, one by one, and paid our bills. The "opposition," the rival networks, were no doubt very far from deceived. At the door I bumped into Helen.

"Helen," I said, "be absolutely casual. Just turn round and come out with me. The COMELEC girls have walked out of the computer count. Let's get down there."

But Helen was bursting for a pee. I swore her to secrecy and told her again to act natural. I knew, as I waited for her, that the chances of Helen crossing the foyer of the Manila Hotel without meeting a friend were zero. I dithered, frantic with casualness, by the door.

Helen kept her word, though, and only told one other journalist.

The COMELEC count was taking place in public, in a large conference center which was one of the Marcoses' notorious extravagances. When we reached the auditorium there was nothing much to see. The girls, around thirty of them, had got up, taking their disks with them, and simply walked out of the building before anyone realized what was going on. The remaining operators were still in place, but because the girls who had walked out occupied a crucial part of the whole computer system, nothing could be done until they and their software were replaced.

A seething general, Remigio P. Octavio, was outside the auditorium. Helen asked him what had happened. Nothing had happened. "Well, General, there seem to be quite a lot of operators missing."

Nobody was missing, said Remigio. The girls had needed a rest. People in the gallery had been jeering at them, throwing stones and paper darts, and they'd gone outside for a rest. They were upset. The gallery had been full of Communists. And to-morrow, he said, he would make sure there were enough police down here to prevent a recurrence. He would bring in rein-forcements.

"As for the girls," said the general, "they will be back again shortly."

Helen wrote all this down on her pad. When she clicks into her reportorial mode and starts firing questions, it's an impres-sive sight. She laces her sentences with respectful language, and makes a great show of taking down every detail and im-probability. But when somebody is lying to her in the way Remigio P. was, the effect of all this is mockery. I wondered whether the general would realize he was being set up. If I had been him, I would have shot Helen.

The girls had taken refuge in Baclaran Church, and it was there the press corps tracked them down. By now they were said to be very scared at the consequences of their walk-out. They needed all the protection the Church could give them, but they also perhaps needed the protection of the press. Per-haps. Perhaps not. Members of the official teams of observers arrived. There was a great sense that these girls were in extreme danger.

It was the second time that day that I had been in Baclaran Church. In the afternoon it had been jam-packed as Cardinal Sin celebrated mass. Cory had attended. The crowds had spilled out into the churchyard and the street-market nearby. Cardinal Sin had preached a sermon so emphatic in its praise of NAMFREL that he had made its members seem almost saints. Depending on your point of view, they were either heroes or villains. There was no middle ground.

Now the church was about a quarter full. Those who had

heard about the walk-out had come to express their support. To pass the time they sang "*Bayan Ko,*" and when the girls finally came out in front of the high altar the audience burst into applause.

The cameras had been set up long since and there were masses of photographers angling for a shot. The girls were sobbing and terrified. I could hardly bear to watch the grilling they got. Their spokeswoman said that they would not give their names, and that it was to be understood that what they had done was not political. They were not in fact (although we called them the COMELEC girls) officials of COMELEC. They were computer operators, highly qualified, who had been engaged to perform what they had taken to be a strictly professional job. All had gone well until the night before, when they began to be instructed not to feed in certain figures, so that the tally board giving the overall position was now at odds with what they knew to be the actual total so far.

I remember the word that was used. Discrepancies. Certain discrepancies had crept in, and the girls were worried by them. Finally they had decided that they were being asked to act unprofessionally. They had come out, and they had brought print-outs and disks with them, in order to prove their case.

Earlier that evening the international team of observers had given a press conference at which John Hume, from Northern Ireland, had been the spokesman. He had been adamant that there had been cheating on the part of the KBL, but he had purposely left open the question of whether that cheating had been on such a scale as to alter the eventual result of the election. The reason he had done this was that people feared Marcos might declare the election null and void, using the evidence of the foreign observers. Marcos was still president. He hadn't needed to call the snap election. If he now annulled it he could, constitutionally, go on as if nothing had happened.

Now the COMELEC girls had come out with the most authoritative evidence of cheating so far. People had been killed for much, much smaller offenses. The Americans could not possibly overlook this evidence, I thought. There would be no getting around it. That was why the girls were in such danger.

One of the American reporters said to the girls that of course they were entitled to withhold their names, but that if they did so Marcos would claim they had not come from COMELEC at all, that this was just black propaganda. For their sakes, they should tell us their names.

At which another pressman snapped, "It's not for their sakes. You just want to get a good story."

The press conference drew to a close. I was thinking: So many people have gone so far – they're so exposed – that the Cory campaign must move forward. If it grinds to a halt now, all these people are just going to be killed.

A figure came rushing into the church. It was the Jesuit from Pasay Town Hall, the one who had been so entertained by Marcos. He came up through the press. "It's very important," he said, "it's very important. They *must* give their names. They *must* give their names."

But the conference was already over, and the girls had gone into hiding.

DAVID QUAMMEN

✖

The Same River Twice

I'VE BEEN READING Heraclitus this week, so naturally my
brain is full of river water.

Heraclitus, you'll recall, was the Greek philosopher of the
sixth century B.C. who gets credit for having said: "You cannot
step twice into the same river." Heraclitus was a loner, according
to the sketchy accounts of him, and rather a crank. He lived in
the town of Ephesus, near the coast of Asia Minor opposite
mainland Greece, not far from a great river that in those days
was called the Meander. He never founded a philosophic school,
as Plato and Pythagoras did. He didn't want followers. He simply wrote his one book and deposited the scroll in a certain
sacred building, the temple of Artemis, where the general
public couldn't get hold of it. The book itself was eventually
lost, and all that survives of it today are about a hundred frag-
ments, which have come down secondhand in the works of
other ancient writers. So his ideas are known only by hearsay.
He seems to have said a lot of interesting things, some of them
cryptic, some of them downright ornery, but his river comment
is the one for which Heraclitus is widely remembered. The full
translation is: "You cannot step twice into the same river, for
other waters are continually flowing on." To most people it

comes across as a nice resonant metaphor, a bit of philosophic poetry. To me it is that and more.

Once, for a stretch of years, I lived in a very small town on the bank of a famous Montana river. It was famous mainly for its trout, for its clear water and its abundance of chemical nutrients, and for the seasonal blizzards of emerging insects that made it one of the most rewarding pieces of habitat in North America, arguably in the world, if you happened to be a trout- or fly-fisherman. I happened to be a fly-fisherman.

One species of insect in particular – one "hatch," to use the slightly misleading term that fishermen apply to these impressive entomological events, when a few billion members of some May fly or Stone fly or Caddis fly species all emerge simultaneously into adulthood and take a flight over a river – one insect hatch in particular gave this river an unmatched renown. The species was *Pteronarcys californica*, a monstrous but benign stone fly that grew more than two inches long, and carried a pinkish-orange underbelly for which it had gotten the common name "salmon fly." These insects, during their three years of development as aquatic larvæ, could only survive in a river that was cold, pure, fast-flowing, rich in dissolved oxygen, and covered across its bed with boulders the size of bowling balls, among which the larvæ would live and graze. The famous river offered all those conditions extravagantly, and so *P. californica* flourished there, like nowhere else. Trout flourished in turn.

When the clouds of *P. californica* took flight, and mated in air, and then began dropping back onto the water, the fish fed upon them voraciously, recklessly. Wary old brown trout the size of a person's thigh, granddaddy animals that would never otherwise condescend to feed by daylight upon floating insects, came off the bottom for this banquet. Each gulp of *P. californica* was a major nutritional windfall. The trout filled their bellies and their mouths and still continued gorging. Consequently the so-called salmon fly so-called hatch on this river, occurring annually during two weeks in June, triggered by small changes in water temperature, became a wild and garish national festival in the fly-fishing year. Stockbrokers in New York, corporate lawyers in San Francisco, federal judges and star-quality surgeons and foundation presidents – the sort of folk who own antique bamboo fly rods and field jackets of Irish tweed – planned their vacations around this event. They packed their gear and then waited for the telephone signal from a guide in a shop on Main Street of the little town where I lived.

The signal would say: *It's started.* Or, in more detail: *Yeah, the hatch is on. Passed through town yesterday. Bugs everywhere. By now the head end of it must be halfway to Varney Bridge. Get here as soon as you can.* They got there. Cabdrivers and schoolteachers came, too. People who couldn't afford to hire a guide and be chauffeured comfortably in a Mackenzie boat, or who didn't want to, arrived with dinghies and johnboats lashed to the roofs of old yellow buses. And if the weather held, and you got yourself to the right stretch of the river at the right time, it could indeed be very damn good fishing.

But that wasn't why I lived in the town. Truth be known, when *P. californica* filled the sky and a flotilla of boats filled the river, I usually headed in the opposite direction. I didn't care for the crowds. It was almost as bad as the Fourth-of-July rodeo, when the town suddenly became clogged with college kids from a nearby city, and Main Street was ankle-deep in beer cans on the morning of the fifth, and I would find people I didn't know sleeping it off in my front yard, under the scraggly elm. The salmon fly hatch was like that, only with stockbrokers and flying hooks. Besides, there were other places and other ways to catch fish. I would take my rod and my waders and disappear to a small spring creek that ran through a stock ranch on the bottomland east of the river.

It was private property. There was no room for guided boats on this little creek, and there was no room for tweed. Instead of tweed there were sheep – usually about 30 head, bleating in halfhearted annoyance but shuffling out of my way as I hiked from the barn out to the water. There was an old swayback horse named Buck, a buckskin; also a younger one, a hot white-stockinged mare that had once been a queen of the barrel-racing circuit and hadn't forgotten her previous station in life. There was a graveyard of rusty car bodies, a string of them, DeSotos and Fords from the Truman years, dumped into the spring creek along one bend to hold the bank in place and save the sheep pasture from turning into an island. Locally this sort of thing is referred to as the "Detroit riprap" mode of soil conservation; after a while, the derelict cars come to seem a harmonious part of the scenery. There was also an old two-story ranch house of stucco, with yellow trim. Inside lived two people, a man and a woman, married then.

Now we have come to the reason I did live in that town. Actually there wasn't one reason but three: the spring creek, the man, and the woman. At the time, for a stretch of years, those were three of the closest friends I'd ever had.

This spring creek was not one of the most eminent Montana spring creeks, not Nelson Spring Creek and not Armstrong, not the sort of place where you could plunk down $25 per rod per day for the privilege of casting your fly over large savvy trout along an exclusive and well-manicured section of water. On this creek you fished free or not at all. I fished free, because I knew the two people inside the house and, through them, the wonderful, surly old rancher who owned the place.

They lived there themselves, those two, in large part because of the creek. The male half of the partnership was at that time a raving and insatiable fly-fisherman, like me, for whom the luxury of having this particular spring creek just a three-minute stroll from his back door was worth any number of professional and personal sacrifices. He had found a place he loved dearly, and he wanted to stay. During previous incarnations he had been a wire-service reporter in Africa, a bar owner in Chicago, a magazine editor in New York, a reform-school guard in Idaho, and a timber-faller in the winter woods of Montana. He had decided to quit the last before he cut off a leg with his chainsaw, or worse; he was later kind enough to offer me his saw and his expert coaching and then to dissuade me deftly from making use of either, during the period when I was so desperate and foolhardy as to consider trying to earn a living that way. All we both wanted, really, was to write novels and fly-fish for trout. We fished the spring creek, together and individually, more than a hundred days each year. We memorized that water. The female half of the partnership, on the other hand, was a vegetarian by principle who lived chiefly on grapefruit and considered that anyone who tormented innocent fish — either for food or, worse, for the sport of catching them and then gently releasing them, as we did — showed the most inexcusable symptoms of arrested development and demented adolescent cruelty, but she tolerated us. All she wanted was to write novels and read Jane Austen and ride the hot mare. None of us had any money.

None of us was being published. Nothing happened in that town between October and May. The man and I played chess. We endangered our lives hilariously cutting and hauling firewood. We skied into the backcountry carrying tents and cast-iron skillets and bottles of wine, then argued drunkenly about whether it was proper to litter the woods with eggshells, if the magpies and crows did it, too. We watched Willie Stargell win a World Series. Sometimes on cold, clear days we put on wool gloves with no fingertips and went out to fish. Meanwhile the woman sequestered herself in a rickety backyard shed, with a small wood stove and a cot and a manual typewriter, surrounded by black widow spiders that she chose to view as pets. Or the three of us stood in their kitchen, until the late hours on winter nights, while the woman peeled and ate uncountable grapefruits and the man and I drank whiskey, and we screamed at each other about literature.

The spring creek ran cool in summer. It ran warm in winter. This is what spring creeks do; this is their special felicity. It steamed and it rippled with fluid life when the main river was frozen over solid. Anchor ice never formed on the rocks of its riffles, killing insect larvæ where they lived, and frazil ice never made the water slushy — as occurred on the main river. During spring runoff, this creek didn't flood; therefore the bottom wasn't scoured and disrupted, and the eggs of the rainbow trout, which spawned around that time, weren't swept out of the nests or buried lethally in silt. The creek did go brown with turbidity, during runoff, from the discharge of several small tributaries that carried meltwater out of the mountains through an erosional zone, but the color would clear again soon.

Insects continued hatching on this creek through the coldest months of the winter. In October and November, large brown trout came upstream from the main river and scooped out their spawning nests on a bend that curved around the sheep pasture, just downstream from the car bodies. In August, grass-hoppers blundered onto the water from the brushy banks, and fish exploded out of nowhere to take them. Occasionally I or the other fellow would cast a tiny fly and pull in a grayling, that gorgeous and delicate cousin of trout, an Arctic species left behind by the last glaciation, that fared poorly in the warm summer temperatures of sun-heated meltwater rivers. In this creek a grayling could be comfortable, because most of the water came from deep underground. That water ran cool in summer, relatively, and warm in winter, relatively – relative in each case to the surrounding air temperature, as well as the temperature of the main river. In absolute terms the creek's temperature tended to be stable year-round, holding steady in a hospitable middle range close to the constant temperature of the ground-water from which it was fed. This is what spring creeks, by definition, do. The scientific jargon for such a balanced condition is *stenothermal:* temperatures in a narrow range. The ecological result is a stable habitat and a 12-month growing season. Free from extremes of cold or heat, free from flooding, free from ice and heavy siltation and scouring, the particular spring creek in question seemed always to me a thing of sublime and succoring constancy. In that regard it was no different from other spring creeks; but it was the one I knew and cared about.

The stretch of years came to an end. The marriage came to an end. There were reasons, but the reasons were private, and

are certainly none of our business here. Books were pulled
down off shelves and sorted into two piles. Fine oaken furniture, too heavy to be hauled into uncertain futures, was sold
off for the price of a sad song. The white-stockinged mare was
sold also, to a family with a couple of young barrel-racers, and
the herd of trap-lame and half-feral cats was divided up. The
man and the woman left town individually, in separate trucks,
at separate times, each headed back toward New York City. I
helped load the second truck, the man's, but my voice wasn't
functioning well on that occasion. I was afflicted with a charley
horse of the throat. It had all been hard to witness, not simply
because a marriage had ended but even more so because, in my
unsolicited judgment, a great love affair had. This partnership
of theirs had been a vivid and imposing thing.

Or maybe it was hard because two love affairs had ended – if
you count mine with the pair of them. I should say here that a
friendship remains between me and each of them. Friendship
with such folk is a lot. But it's not the same.

Now I live in the city from which college students flock off to
the Fourth-of-July rodeo in that little town, where they raise
hell for a day and litter Main Street with beer cans and then
sleep it off under the scraggly elm in what is now someone else's
front yard – the compensation being that July Fourth is quieter
up here. It is only an hour's drive. Not too long ago I was down
there myself.

I parked, as always, in the yard by the burn barrel outside
the stucco house. The house was empty; I avoided it. With my
waders and my fly rod I walked out to the spring creek. Of
course it was all a mistake.

I stepped into the creek and began fishing my way upstream,
casting a grasshopper imitation into patches of shade along the
overhung banks. There were a few strikes. There was a fish
caught and released. But after less than an hour I quit. I
climbed out of the water. I left. I had imagined that a spring
creek was a thing of sublime and succoring constancy. I was
wrong. Heraclitus was right.

JOHN HAINES

✖

Shadows

I

THERE ARE SHADOWS over the land. They come out of the
ground, from the dust and the tumbled bones of the earth.
Tree shadows that haunt the woodlands of childhood, holding
fear in their branches. Stone shadows on the desert, cloud
shadows on the sea and over the summer hills, bringing water.
Shapes of shadow in pools and wells, vague forms in the sand-
light.

Out of the past come these wind-figures, the flapping sails
of primitive birds with terrible beaks and claws. Shadows of
things that walked once and went away. Lickers of blood that
fasten by night to the veins of standing cattle, to the foot of a
sleeping man. In the Far North, the heavy, stalled bodies of
mastodons chilled in a black ooze, and their fur-clad bones still
come out of the ground. Triceratops was feeding in the marsh-
lands by the verge of the coal-making forest.

Shadows in doorways, and under the eaves of ancient buildings, where the fallen creatures of stone grimace in sleep.
Domestic, wind-tugged shadows cast by icy branches upon a
bedroom window: they tap on the glass and wake us. They
speak to the shadows within us, old ghosts that will not die. Like
trapped, primordial birds, they break from an ice-pool in the
heart's well and fly into walls built long ago.

Stand still where you are — at the end of pavement, in a sun-break of the forest, on the open, cloud-peopled terrace of the plains. Look deeply into the wind-furrows of the grass, into the leaf-stilled water of pools. Think back through the silence, of the life that was and is not here now, of the strong pastness of things – shadows of the end and the beginning.

It is autumn. Leaves are flying, a storm of them over the land. They are brown and yellow, parched and pale – Shelley's "pestilence-stricken multitudes." Out of an evening darkness they fly in our faces and scare us; like resigned spirits they whirl away and spill into hollows, to lie still, one on the other, waiting for snow.

II

I STEPPED OUT into my yard on a warm October evening, just before dark. I forget now why I had gone out – perhaps for an armload of wood, or to check on the last of the sunset and the oncoming night sky. In those days, when I was done with eating and sleeping, the natural place for me to be was outdoors.

I hadn't been out long when I saw what at first I thought was a large, dark leaf blowing toward me in the dusk. But there was no wind. Like a silent and tumbling leaf it brushed by me and disappeared behind the house. Moments later it returned, darting erratically overhead, and again it dropped from sight, this time down the road toward the river. It occurred to me that it might be a late swallow, but it seemed too dark, silent, and strange, and so far as I knew all swallows had long since left the country.

Again the strange visitor fluttered past me in the semi-darkness. And suddenly I knew that this swift, wayward, climbing and falling thing was a bat, that there must be more than one flying in the dusk around me. As the fall evening slowly edged into night, I stood still and watched.

It was impossible to keep track of them in that dim light. As soon as I had one fixed in flight against the sky, it veered off into the darkness of the trees and vanished. The bats flew with a queer, jerky movement – a flight somewhat like that of a butterfly, but stronger and swifter. It was as if, out of the still evening air in which they flew, a sudden and unfelt gust of wind snatched them aside; or that at any moment they felt the limit of an invisible string that yanked them from their path.

I knew nothing of bats. Never before had one come to the yard, and never in many evening walks to the river had I seen a bat near the water. I knew only this swift, buoyant flight in the dusk, the mysteriousness of their late appearance in a country from which all other summer creatures had gone. In a kind of spell I watched them for as long as I could distinguish any movement in the darkness. The fall night closed over the landscape, leaving a few stray gleams of light on the river, and I went back indoors.

Looking among the nature guides on the bookshelf, I found a section on bats and began reading. I learned that the earliest fossil bat has been dated back to the Eocene, ninety-five million years after the first bird flapped through the Jurassic skies, and long after the last flying reptiles had become part of the earth's stone history. The teeth and skulls of fossil bats are similar to those of early monkeys, suggesting a common ancestor. And the writer went on to say that bats may be among our earliest relatives.

Only two kinds of bats were found in the Far North, and in Alaska these were thought to inhabit a region two or three hundred miles farther south. But obviously that information was incorrect. I soon decided, from my reading and from what I had been able to observe of their size and flight habits, that the bats I had seen were the *Little Brown Myotis*, one of the smallest and commonest of North American bats. They belonged to a widespread family of insect-feeding bats, having a body no larger than that of a meadow mouse, with a wingspread of perhaps ten inches. I read that they were colonial in their habits; that some individuals hibernated during the winter, while others migrated; that they slept by day in caves, in old buildings and hollow trees. In deep dusk they could be seen flying near water and at the edge of the forest. And what I was reading seemed to be true, for here they were, hunting my cleared spaces among the birches.

The next evening I walked up the highway to the mailbox to post a letter. Again the evening was still and warm, with an occasional light air moving over the hills and a deep gold light on the river channel in the southwest. I soon saw a bat flying up and down the roadway, back and forth, swiftly changing altitude in pursuit of the insects that were still abroad. More than once it vanished among the trees bordering the roadside, to reappear as a tumbling, leaf-shaped thing against the clear night sky.

It seemed to me as I walked, my attention held by the constant surprise of its flight, that the bat in turn was attracted by my passage on the road. It brushed by me, and abruptly out of the hovering darkness it swooped over my head and flew before me up the road. I felt oddly comforted, exhilarated by the nearness of this unique and searching creature in the dusk. When I returned from the mailbox, the bat again seemed to accompany me – as if, in obedience to some obscure purpose in life, it too delighted in the companionship.

The warm weather held for another day or two, and then with that swiftness of deepening fall the days and nights turned cold. I did not see the bats again that year.

Thinking on their sudden appearance and swift departure, I wondered where they had gone. Had they really flown south, far south, carried aloft by that delicate membrane stretched between wrist and foot? It seemed to me unlikely that they could pass the mountains through Canada, or survive the coastline and the stormy Gulf. Even so, I imagined them making their way somehow, flitting from corridor to corridor, dependent on the insects still awake in that uncertain latitude.

Or had they found a crevice in a nearby rockface, some earth-warmed cavern, and deep in that shelter drawn in upon themselves whatever warmth their small bodies possessed, and gone to sleep for the winter?

I was not to know the answers to my questions. As the days shortened, I thought of the bats from time to time, wondering what it would be like to be with them, wherever they were, clinging head-down in sleep to a precarious edge, waiting for spring – perhaps to freeze and never awake.

"Bats have few enemies. Bad weather is one of them. When not hibernating, they seem unable to endure long fasts; protracted cold, windy, rainy weather that keeps insects from flying, causes considerable mortality...."*

For the rest of us plodding terrestrial creatures, snow came soon, and the year plunged deeper into frost.

THE FOLLOWING YEAR in late September I hiked down into Banner Creek from Campbell's Hill on my way home from hunting. Halfway down the open hillside I stopped briefly to look inside a dilapidated frame shack left behind by miners a few years before. It was nearly dusk, and the light inside the shack was poor. But as my eyes became accustomed to the gloom, I found that I was not alone in the shack. My attention was caught by a dark, rounded shape on the wall near a window, halfway up from the floor. I stepped quietly over to it and found a small brown bat clinging to a crack in one of the boards. I had no light with me, and I was unable to see clearly any details of the creature, but it seemed to me that it was awake and that a pair of bright, steady eyes was watching me. I had a momentary impulse to pick the bat up and carry it outside where I could have a better look at it. I decided not to disturb it. I might have learned more, but I felt that it would not be worth the risk of scaring or injuring the bat.

After a brief search of the bare room, and finding no other bats, I left the shack and quietly shut the door. The door had been closed when I came, and the bat had apparently entered through a hole in the eaves or by a broken windowpane.

* Henry Hill Collins, Jr., *Complete Field Guide to North American Wildlife*. Harper & Brothers, New York, 1958, p. 267.

A week and some days later a pair of bats once again came to the homestead yard on a mild evening and flew about, as they had the year before, until long after dark. And again, when the period of warm evenings ended, they disappeared.

They visited the homestead in this way for about four years. They came once or twice in late summer, but more often in the fall when a south wind had blown the last leaves from the birches, when the woods were silent and waiting. That rare, mild evening came, a few insects – moths and gnats – emerged, and the dusk took on its brief summer life again.

Then, as mysteriously as they had first appeared, the bats deserted the homestead. I do not remember having seen them before that time, and not often since. During that same four-year period there were scattered reports of bats seen near Fairbanks in the evenings by people who did not know they existed so far north. It is likely that in milder years since then these small bats have come and gone in other neighborhoods, mostly unnoticed by people in lighted houses.

It may have been that from time to time a change in the climate of the Interior, so slight that it was otherwise unmarked, extended their range northward; or that a subtle shift in the pattern of their local migration brought them to the river, to the yard and the open field above it. And then, like so many other events in our lives, perhaps no explanation is required. A wind from a great, hidden tree blew in our direction one evening and, like leaves loosened from a shaken bough, they came and they vanished.

Despite the shadowy undertones of folk literature and old wives' tales – the imagery of fear and transformation, of witchcraft and brooms, and despite what I remembered from childhood of my mother's and grandmother's alarm at the very thought of having a bat in the house – I have never felt uneasiness in their presence. I remember an incident years ago when I was a student in Washington. I came home late one night to the roominghouse where I lived; as I climbed to the landing on the second floor, I saw a large bat flying up and down the corridor. It flew swiftly, avoiding me each time it passed. The mid-fall evening was warm, and the bat may have been attracted by the moths that were fluttering at the landing light. I was concerned that the bat would be trapped and injured, and before going upstairs to my room I opened a window at one end of the corridor.

"They are not witches....They will not try to get into your hair. Like most animals and some people, what they want is to be left alone."*

Though surely indifferent to our presence, as all wild things tend to be, they seemed to me in that far northern place, at the uttermost limit of their range – remote from attics and belfries, from all folklore and superstition; remote from every human infringement that has so often determined the existence of their kind – to be warm, curious, and friendly creatures whose lives momentarily touch our own.

Another and distant fall shed its leaves in the wind; no bats came, and something of that rare kinship was missing in the October evening.

III

I SPEAK MUCH of twilight, of dusk and evening. I began with shadows and I must end with them, having lighted a clearing along the way. To go farther is to describe a persistence of the forest and its shadows within us. How the man-beast of fantasy and star-crossed resemblance returns, as dream image clothed in scales, feathers, and fur; in those confused reaffirmations of transitional life – werewolves and vampires, blood-drinking night-things with sharp teeth and pointed ears.

The imagery of early art and literature is rich in representations of men who have put on the hair and strength, the fierceness and courage, of the lion, bull, and bear, the fleetness of the deer, and the eyesight of the eagle. Related figures, ranked

* *Ibid.*, p. 298.

in the lower orders of fox and ferret, assume characteristics of deceit and thievish cunning. Bats displayed on the coats of arms of old families in Britain were meant to show traits of watchfulness and wakefulness. A bat emblem signified a man of quick and secret execution.

A debased form of this identification speaks to us today in the vocabulary of the sports pages, in the labels distributed among items of manufacture, in the names often given to weapons of warfare to suggest a threatening and fearless aspect; and in those comic but predatory cartoon figures of batmen and wolfmen who flourish in the atmosphere of another, more fantastic planet where the mind roams at will among inherited images.

Examples of blood-identity, of remedies and safeguards, cram the histories. An ancient proverb concerning madness tells us that "he who eats the heart or tongue of a bat shall flee from water and die." A bat tied to the left arm will keep away sleep. A bat carried three times around a house and nailed head-down above the doorway will bar misfortune. The heads of young bats and swallows, pounded and mixed with honey, will improve dim vision. And if you should be so fortunate as to see anything hidden, submerged in darkness, anoint your face with the blood of a bat, and you may read by night.

An early explorer in Australia was warned not to kill a bat, for it was "brother belonging to black fellow." In colonial Mexico an old woman one day complained to two priests of their abuse of her. When in astonishment they protested, she reminded them that the day before they had chased a bat from their house. "I was that bat," the old woman said, "and now I am exhausted."

Lodged in batlore are the souls changed by sleep, who are never seen in daylight when men are awake. So, in deposits of slate fifty million years old, lie the remains of fossil bats, sound in their stony sleep, who will awaken when the oceans rise and unending night claims the earth.

Somewhere in Christian folklore the story is told of how Jesus, retired to seclusion in the mountains and cut off from a view of the desert, made a clay image of a winged creature and breathed upon it. And immediately it opened its wings and fled into a cavern in the mountains. Thereafter it emerged every night at sunset to tell him of the close of day.

The Maya Kingdom of Darkness was ruled by Camazotz, the death-bat. Representations show the god in human form with bat-like wings, the nose-leaf shaped to a stone knife with which he slays his victims. A stream of blood flows from the god's mouth to signify the destruction of life and devouring of darkness.

An outpouring of images, as numerous, as filled with voices as a colony of bats issuing from a desert cave on its nightly search. The awakened bats swarm above the thornbrush, and in the steep light of dusk an echo comes back to us ten million years after the sound was uttered and the mouth is dust.

BEFORE KNOWLEDGE there was wisdom, grounded in the shadows of a dimly lit age. We ourselves have been night creatures, and once the human soul left its sleeping body, to soar and feed nightlong in the shape of a bat or exotic bird, returning to the sleeper at daybreak.

Turn out all the lights in your town or city, and see how swiftly life returns to the shadows, how soon from within unlit trees and from silent doorways the ancient dread comes back, and night is once more filled with snouts and whispers, with leathery wings, and heavy bodies colliding.

The attitudes flicker and change, rehearsed continually on the screen of the wind. To be merely a creature on earth, to be left alone in an acre of grass, has seldom been sufficient – not since man the hunter scanned the open fairway, crouched in ambush, and took passionately to himself the skins of killed beasts, tore their meat from the bones, drank their milk and blood, and then by torchlight traced their outlines on a high rockface in soot and ochre.

As if fed by necessity, by intuition that blood indeed moves the sun, and is the sun's energy reddened and intensified in the human heart, imagination chooses its victims in an act of perpetual sacrifice. It seizes upon the wild creature and turns it into an image of some interior force we feel but cannot see, be it god or demon.

It is as though we require that evil exist, and that we find its faces in the world. A potential harm animates the expressions of certain animals – a menace in the wet lips drawn back on the gleaming teeth, as in the strange, thirsty little muzzles of bats and shrews. So a silent terror accompanies the predatory armor and clicking mandibles of beetles – all that, in the grass world beneath us, in the water world and leaf world around us, signifies the relentless stalking of an insect prey.

In spite of all subsequent knowledge, the outcome of "objective," "detached" observation, something fixed in the soul finds satisfaction in these images of cunning and ferocity. We respond to a sound in the syllables of certain words and phrases: "the Wolf of the Air, and the Wolf of the Pond." The grimaces, the frozen smiles, the wind-snarls of the spirit-faces cut into the eroding stone of temples and stelæ, contain our loves, our hates, and our angers. In that mysterious logic of totemic art, the monstrous carved and painted guardians posted before the law and the household preserved for those within a precarious peace.

We misread these images if we think of them as horrible and frightening only, for the harm they seem to threaten. For behind that immediate and apparent violence they are as well, and perhaps above all, images of a lost and intenser being. Standing erect in polished bronze, Yamakanda, a many-armed Tibetan god, clutches his consort in what appears to be a ferocious and devouring embrace. But that embrace can be understood as an expression of devotion and love, and the terrible, wrinkling smile that accompanies it is formed with the only face the beast-god has to wear.

And still that lost being pursues us, no matter how remote and abstract our sensibilities have become. The mark of the forest is on us, never to be burned away. Upon the capitals of pillars in the chapterhouses of old churches in Europe the staring likenesses of lords and kings have been carved, their foreheads clenched and bitten by swine-headed creatures, by harpies and scaled dragons whose taloned and beaked reality often seems more real than any clinical terms we can assign to pain, disorder, and sorrow. In the final canto of Dante's *Inferno*, Satan appears as a huge, half-frozen bat-like being whose wings, opening and closing, fan a great frost and send forth the world's evil. A lasting grief rolls down those towering and blackened features in tears of ice.

And then, released from an old grip of terror, and with nothing but the familiar woodland of rain, leaf, and sunlight to walk through, the haunted, legendary features dissolve, and we see only another being on earth – a bounding bundle of red fur, a burst of gray feathers – as bound to necessity as ourselves.

And of the bats at Richardson, whose brown leaf-shapes crossed the twilight at such rare intervals, to speak now and then of companionship and delight is sufficient, for these may be found anywhere in the pure act of being, of pursuing one's way by daylight and dusk, filling by right that clearing, that space of air, that acre of soil and grass, undeflected by regret or thought of tomorrow.

The weather changes, the ice retreats or advances; drought and rain alternate as the continents slide and the chill vectors shift north or south. The woods vanish before the axe, the saw, and the plow; they reappear when the handgrip relaxes. Shadows disperse to the outskirts of our lighted settlements, and the heavy smoke-dimmed dusk is voiceless.

I walk by the roadside, looking into the strong west light. The air is warm and the wind is gentle. A late swarm of gnats blows up from somewhere in the roadside brush. They hover before me, give way and reassemble behind me. They remind me of past evenings, of shadows, whispers, and vanished companions. However things may be elsewhere in this calm autumn world, there are no bats flying above the roadway this evening.

AND TO THINK, from this long vista of empty light and deepening shade, that so small and refined a creature could fill an uncertain niche in the world; and that its absence would leave not just a momentary gap in nature, but a lack in one's own existence, one less possibility of being.

As if we were to look out on a cherished landscape, hoping to see on the distant, wrinkled plain, among the cloud shadows passing over its face, groups of animals feeding and resting; and in the air above them a compact flock of waterfowl swiftly beating its way to a farther pond; and higher still, a watchful hawk on the wind. To look, straining one's eyes, noting each detail of lake, meadow, and bog; and to find nothing, nothing alive and moving. Only the wind and the distance, the silence of a vast, creatureless earth.

1975-1985

PATRICIA HAMPL

✖

Parish Streets

LEXINGTON, OXFORD, Chatsworth, continuing down Grand Avenue to Milton and Avon, as far as St. Albans – the streets of our neighborhood had an English, even an Anglican, ring to them. But we were Catholic, and the parishes of the diocese, unmarked and ghostly as they were, posted borders more decisive than the street signs we passed on our way to St. Luke's grade school or, later, walking in the other direction to Visitation Convent for high school.

We were like people with dual citizenship. I *lived* on Linwood Avenue, but I *belonged* to St. Luke's. That was the lingo. Mothers spoke of daughters who were going to the junior-senior prom with boys "from Nativity" or "from St. Mark's," as if from feifdoms across the sea.

"Where you from?" a boy livid with acne asked when we startled each other lurking behind a pillar in the St. Thomas Academy gym at a Friday night freshman mixer.

"Ladies' choice!" one of the mothers cried from a dim corner where a portable hi-fi was set up. She rasped the needle over the vinyl, and Fats Domino came on, insinuating a heavier pleasure than I yet knew: *I found my thrill…on Blueberry Hill.*

"I'm from Holy Spirit," the boy said, as if he'd been beamed in to stand by the tepid Cokes and tuna sandwiches and the bowls of sweating potato chips on the refreshments table.

Parish members did not blush to describe themselves as being "from Immaculate Conception." Somewhere north, near the city line, there was even a parish frankly named Maternity of Mary. But then, in those years, the 1950s and early 1960s, breeding was a low-grade fever pulsing amongst us unmentioned, like a buzz or hum you get used to and cease to hear. The white noise of matrimonial sex.

On Sundays the gray stone nave of St. Luke's church, big as a warehouse, was packed with families of eight or ten sitting in the honey-colored pews. The fathers wore brown suits. In memory they appear spectrally thin, wraithlike and spent, like trees hollowed of their pulp. The wives were petite and cheerful with helmet-like haircuts. Perkiness was their main trait. But what did they say, these small women, how did they talk? Mrs. Healy, mother of fourteen ("They can afford them," my mother said, as if to excuse her paltry two. "He's a doctor."), never uttered a word, as far as I remember. Even pregnant, she was somehow wiry, as if poised for a tennis match. Maybe these women only wore a *look* of perkiness, and like their lean husbands, they were sapped of personal strength. Maybe they were simply tense.

Not everyone around us was Catholic. Mr. Kirby, a widower who was our next door neighbor, was Methodist – whatever that was. The Nugents across the street behind their cement retaining wall and double row of giant salvia, were Lutheran, more or less. The Williams family, who subscribed to the *New Yorker* and had a living room outfitted with spare Danish furniture, were Episcopalian. They referred to their minister as a priest – a plagiarism that embarrassed me for them because I liked them and their light, airy ways.

As for the Bertrams, our nearest neighbors to the west, it could only be said that Mrs. Bertram, dressed in a narrow suit with a peplum jacket and a hat made of the same heathery wool, went *somewhere* via taxi on Sunday mornings. Mr. Bertram went nowhere – on Sunday or on any other day. He was understood, during my entire girlhood, to be indoors, resting.

Weekdays, Mrs. Bertram took the bus to her job downtown.

Mr. Bertram stayed home behind their birchwood Venetian blinds in an aquarium half-light, not an invalid (we never thought of him that way), but a man whose occupation it was to rest. Sometimes in the summer he ventured forth with a large wrench-like gadget to root out the masses of dandelions that gave the Bertram lawn a temporary brilliance in June.

I associated him with the Wizard of Oz. He was small and mild-looking, going bald. He gave the impression of extreme pallor except for small, very dark eyes.

It was a firm neighborhood rumor that Mr. Bertram had been a screenwriter in Hollywood. Yes, that pallor was a writer's pallor; those small dark eyes were a writer's eyes. They saw, they noted.

He allowed me to assist him in the rooting-out of his dandelions. I wanted to ask him about Hollywood — had he met Audrey Hepburn? I couldn't bring myself to manœver for information on such an important subject. But I did feel something serious was called for here. I introduced religion while he plunged the dandelion gadget deep into the lawn.

No, he said, he did not go to church. "But you do believe in God?" I asked, hardly daring to hope he did not. I longed for novelty.

He paused for a moment and looked up at the sky where big, spreading clouds streamed by. "God isn't the problem," he said.

Some ancient fissure split open, a fine crack in reality: so there *was* a problem. Just as I'd always felt. Beneath the family solidity, the claustrophobia of mother-father-brother-me, past the emphatic certainties of St. Luke's catechism class, there was a problem that would never go away. Mr. Bertram stood amid his dandelions, resigned as a Buddha, looking up at the sky which gave back nothing but drifting white shapes on the blue.

What alarmed me was my feeling of recognition. Of course there was a problem. It wasn't God. Life itself was a problem. Something was not right, would never be right. I'd sensed it all along, some kind of fishy vestigial quiver in the spine. It was bred in the bone, way past thought. Life, deep down, lacked the substantiality that it *seemed* to display. The physical world, full of detail and interest, was a parched topsoil that could be blown away.

This lack, this blankness akin to chronic disappointment, was everywhere, under the perkiness, lurking even within my own happiness. "What are you going to do today?" my father said when he saw me digging in the backyard on his way to work at the greenhouse.

"I'm digging to China," I said.

"Well, I'll see you at lunch," he said, "if you're still here."

I wouldn't bite. I frowned and went back to work with the bent tablespoon my mother had given me. It wasn't a game. I wanted out. I was on a desperate journey that only looked like play. I couldn't explain.

The blank disappointment, masked as weariness, played on the faces of people on the St. Clair bus. They looked out the windows, coming home from downtown, unseeing: clearly nothing interested them. What were they thinking of? The passing scene was not beautiful enough — was that it? — to catch their eye. Like the empty clouds Mr. Bertram turned to, their blank looks gave back nothing. There was an unshivered shiver in each of us, a shudder we managed to hold back.

We got off the bus at Oxford where, one spring, in the lime green house behind the catalpa tree on the corner, Mr. Lenart (whom we didn't know well) had slung a pair of tire chains over a rafter in the basement and hanged himself. Such things happened. Only the tight clutch of family life ("The family that prays together stays together.") could keep things rolling along. Step out of the tight, bright circle, and you might find yourself dragging your chains down to the basement.

The perverse insubstantiality of the material world was the problem: reality refused to be real enough. Nothing could keep you steadfastly happy. That was clear. Some people blamed God. But I sensed that Mr. Bertram was right not to take that tack. *God is not the problem.* The clouds passing in the big sky kept dissipating, changing form. That was the problem — but

so what? Such worries resolved nothing, and were best left un-
worried – the unshivered shiver.

There was no one to blame. You could only retire, like Mr.
Bertram, stay indoors behind your birchwood blinds, and contemplate the impossibility of things, allowing the Hollywood
glitter of reality to fade away and become a vague local rumor.

There were other ways of coping. Mrs. Krueger, several houses
down with a big garden rolling with hydrangea bushes, held as
her faith a passionate belief in knowledge. She sold *World Book*
encyclopedias. After trying Christian Science and a stint with
the Unitarians, she had settled down as an agnostic. There
seemed to be a lot of reading involved with being an agnostic,
pamphlets and books, long citations on cultural anthropology
in the *World Book*. It was an abstruse religion, and Mrs. Krueger
seemed to belong to some ladies' auxiliary of disbelief.

But it didn't really matter what Mrs. Krueger decided about
"the deity-idea," as she called God. No matter what they believed, our neighbors lived not just on Linwood Avenue; they
were in St. Luke's parish too, whether they knew it or not. We
claimed the territory. And we claimed them – even as we dismissed them. They were all non-Catholics, the term that dis-
posed nicely of all spiritual otherness.

Let the Protestants go their schismatic ways; the Lutherans
could splice themselves into synods any which way. Believers,
non-believers, even Jews (the Kroners on the corner) or a breed
as rare as the Greek Orthodox whose church was across the
street from St. Luke's – they were all non-Catholics, just so
much extraneous spiritual matter orbiting the nethersphere.

Or maybe it was more intimate than that, and we dismissed
the rest of the world as we would our own serfs. We saw the
Lutherans and Presbyterians, even those snobbish Episcopal-
ians, as rude colonials, non-Catholics all, doing the best they
could out there in the bush to imitate the ways of the homeland.
We were the homeland.

JIMMY GUILIANI was a bully. He pulled my hair when he ran by me on Oxford as we all walked home from St. Luke's, the girls like a midget army in navy jumpers and white blouses, the boys with the greater authority of free civilians without uniforms. They all wore pretty much the same thing anyway: corduroy pants worn smooth at the knees and flannel shirts, usually plaid.

I wasn't the only one Jimmy picked on. He pulled Moira Murphy's hair, he punched Tommy Hague. He struck without reason, indiscriminately, so full of violence it may have been pent-up enthusiasm released at random after the long day leashed in school. Catholic kids were alleged, by public school kids, to be mean fighters, dirty fighters.

Jimmy Guiliani was the worst, a terror, hated and feared by Sister Julia's entire third grade class.

So, it came as a surprise when, after many weeks of his tyranny, I managed to land a sure kick to his groin and he collapsed in a heap and cried real tears. "You shouldn't *do* that to a boy," he said, whimpering. He was almost primly admonishing. "Do you know how that feels?"

It's not correct to say that it was a sure kick. I just kicked. I took no aim and had no idea I'd hit paydirt — or why. Even when the tears started to his eyes and he doubled over clutching himself, I didn't understand.

But I liked it when he asked if I knew how it felt. For a brief, hopeful moment I thought he would tell me, that he would explain. Yes, tell me: how *does* it feel? And what's *there*, anyway? It was the first time the male body imposed itself.

I felt an odd satisfaction. I'd made contact. I wasn't glad I had hurt him, I wasn't even pleased to have taken the group's revenge on the class bully. I hadn't planned to kick him. It all just *happened* — as most physical encounters do. I was more astonished than he that I had succeeded in wounding him, I think. In a simple way, I wanted to say I was sorry. But I liked being taken seriously, and could not forfeit that rare pleasure by making an apology.

For a few weeks after I kicked him, I had a crush on Jimmy Guiliani. Not because I'd hurt him. But because he had paused, looked right at me, and implored me to see things from his point of view. *Do you know how it feels?*

I didn't know – and yet I did. As soon as he asked, I realized obscurely that I did know how it felt. I knew what was there between his legs where he hurt. I ceased to be ignorant at that moment. And sex began – with a blow.

The surprise of knowing what I hadn't realized I knew seemed beautifully private, but also illicit. That was a problem. I had no desire to be an outlaw. The way I saw it, you were supposed to know what you had been *taught*. This involved being given segments of knowledge by someone (usually a nun) designated to dole out information in measured drams, like strong medicine.

Children were clean slates others were meant to write on.

But here was evidence I was not a blank slate at all. I was scribbled all over with intuitions, premonitions, vague resonances clamoring to give their signals. I had caught Mr. Bertram's skyward look and its implicit promise: life will be tough. There was no point in blaming God – the Catholic habit. Or even more Catholic, blaming the nuns, which allowed you to blame Mother and God all in one package.

And here was Jimmy Guiliani drawing out of me this other knowledge, bred of empathy and a swift kick to his privates. *Yes, I know how it feels.*

THE HIERARCHY we lived in, a great linked chain of religious being, seemed set to control every entrance and exit to and from the mind and heart. The buff-colored *Baltimore Catechism*, small and square, read like an owner's manual for a very complicated vehicle. There was something pleasant, lulling and rhythmic, like heavily rhymed poetry, about the sing-song Q-and-A format. Who would not give over heart, if not mind, to the brisk nannyish assurance of the Baltimore prose:

Who made you?
God made me.

Why did God make you?
*God made me to know, love and serve Him in this world, in order to
be happy with Him forever in the next.*

What pleasant lines to commit to memory. And how harmless
our Jesuitical discussions about what, exactly, constituted a
meatless spaghetti sauce on Friday. Strict constructionists said
no meat of any kind should ever, at any time, have made its way
into the tomato sauce; easy liberals held with the notion that
meatballs could be lurking around in the sauce, as long as you
didn't eat them. My brother lobbied valiantly for the meatball
intactus but present. My mother said nothing doing. They raged
for years.

Father Flannery, who owned his own airplane and drove a
sports car, had given Peter some ammunition when he'd been
asked to rule on the meatball question in the confessional. My
mother would hear none of it. "I don't want to know what goes
on between you and your confessor," she said, taking the high
road.

"A priest, Ma, a *priest*," my brother cried. "This is an ordained
priest saying right there in the sanctity of the confessional that
meatballs are OK."

But we were going to heaven my mother's way.

Life was like that – crazy. Full of hair-splitting, and odd rituals. We got our throats blessed on St. Blaise day in February,
with the priest holding oversized bees-wax candles in an X
around our necks, to ward off death by choking on fishbones.
There were smudged foreheads on Ash Wednesday, and home
May altars with plaster statuettes of the Virgin festooned with
lilacs. Advent wreaths and nightly family rosary vigils during
October (Rosary Month), the entire family on their knees in the
living room.

There were snatches of stories about nuns who beat kids with rulers in the coat room; the priest who had a twenty-year affair with a member of the Altar and Rosary Society; the other priest in love with an altar boy – they'd had to send him away. Not St. Luke's stories – oh no, certainly not – but stories, floating, as stories do, from inner ear to inner ear, respecting no parish boundaries. Part of the ether.

And with it all, a relentless xenophobia about other religions. "It's going to be a mixed marriage, I understand," one of my aunts murmured about a friend's daughter who was marrying an Episcopalian. So what if he called himself High Church? What did that change? He was a non-Catholic.

And now, educated out of it all, well climbed into the professions, the Catholics find each other at cocktail parties and get going. The nun stories, the first confession traumas – and a tone of rage and dismay that seems to bewilder even the tellers of these tales.

Nobody says, when asked, "I'm Catholic." It's always, "Yes, I was brought up Catholic." Anything to put it at a distance, to diminish the presence of that grabby heritage that is not racial but acts as if it were. "You never get over it, you know," a fortyish lawyer told me a while ago at a party where we found ourselves huddled by the chips and dip, as if we were at a St. Thomas mixer once again.

He seemed to feel he was speaking to someone with the same hopeless congenital condition. "It's different now, of course," he said. "But when we were growing up back there...." Ah yes, the past isn't a time. It's a place. And it's always there.

He had a very Jimmy Guiliani look to him. A chastened rascal. "I'm divorced," he said. We both smiled: there's no going to hell anymore. "Do they still have mortal sin?" he asked wistfully.

The love-hate lurch of a Catholic upbringing, like having an extra set of parents to contend with. Or an added national allegiance – not to the Vatican, as we were warned that the Baptists thought during John Kennedy's campaign for president. The allegiance was to a different realm. It was the implacable loyalty of faith, that flawless relation between self and existence which we were born into. A strange country where people prayed and believed impossible things.

The nuns who taught us, rigged up in their bold black habits with the big round wimples stiff as frisbees, walked our parish streets; they moved from convent to church in twos or threes, dipping in the side door of the huge church "for a little adoration," as they would say. The roly-poly Irish-born monsignor told us to stand straight and proud when he met us slouching along Summit toward class. And fashionable Father Flannery who, every night, took a gentle, companionable walk with the old Irish pastor, the two of them taking out white handkerchiefs, waving them for safety, as they crossed the busy avenue on the way home in the dark, swallowed in their black suits and cassocks, invisible in the gloom.

But the one I would like to summon up most and to have pass me on Oxford as I head off to St. Luke's in the early morning mist, one of those mid-May weekdays, the lilacs just starting to spill, that one I want most to materialize from "back there" – I don't know her name, where, exactly, she lived, or who she was. We never spoke, in fact. We just passed each other, she coming home from six o'clock daily Mass, I going early to school to practice the piano for an hour before class began.

She was a "parish lady," part of the anonymous population that thickened our world, people who were always there, who were solidly part of us, part of what we were, but who never emerged beyond the bounds of being parishioners to become persons.

We met every morning, just past the Healy's low brick wall. She wore a librarian's cardigan sweater. She must have been about forty-five, and I sensed she was not married. Unlike Dr. and Mrs. Harrigan who walked smartly along Summit holding hands, their bright Irish setter accompanying them as far as the church door where he waited till Mass was over, the lady in the cardigan was always alone.

I saw her coming all the way from Grand where she had to

pause for the traffic. She never rushed across the street, zipping past a truck, but waited until the coast was completely clear, and passed across keeping her slow, almost floating pace. A lovely, peaceful gait, no rush to it.

When finally we were close enough to make eye contact, she looked up, straight into my face, and smiled. It was such a *complete* smile, so entire, that it startled me every time, as if I'd heard my name called out on the street of a foreign city.

She was a homely woman, plain and pale, unnoticeable. But I felt – how to put it – that she shed light. The mornings were often frail with mist, the light uncertain and tender. The smile was a brief flood of light. She loved me, I felt.

I knew what it was about. She was praying. Her hand, stuck in her cardigan pocket, held one of the crystal beads of her rosary. I knew this. I'd once seen her take it out of the left pocket and quickly replace it after she had found the handkerchief she needed.

If I had seen a nun mumbling the rosary along Summit (and that did happen), it would not have meant much to me. But here on Oxford, the side street we used as a sleepy corridor to St. Luke's, it was a different thing. The parish lady was not a nun. She was a person who prayed, who prayed alone, for no reason that I understood. But there was no question that she prayed without ceasing, as the strange scriptural line instructed.

She didn't look up to the blank clouds for a response, as Mr. Bertram did in his stoic way. Her head was bowed, quite unconsciously. And when she raised it, keeping her hand in her pocket where the clear beads were, she looked straight into the eyes of the person passing by. It was not an invasive look, but one brimming with a secret which, if only she had words, it was clear she would like to tell.

WILLIAM KITTREDGE

✖

Drinking and Driving

DEEP IN THE FAR HEART of my upbringing, a crew of us sixteen-year-old lads were driven crazy with ill-defined mid-summer sadness by the damp, sour-smelling sweetness of night-time alfalfa fields, an infinity of stars and moonglow, and no girlfriends whatsoever. Frogs croaked in the lonesome swamp.

Some miles away over the Warner Range was the little ranch and lumbermill town of Lakeview, with its whorehouse district. And I had use of my father's 1949 Buick. So, another summer drive. The cathouses, out beyond the rodeo grounds, were clustered in an area called Hollywood, which seemed right. Singing cowboys were part of everything gone wrong.

We would sink our lives in cheap whiskey and the ardor of sad, expensive women. In town, we circled past the picture show and out past Hollywood, watching the town boys and their town-boy business, and we chickened out on the whores and drank more beer, then drove on through the moonlight.

Toward morning we found ourselves looping higher and higher on a two-truck gravel road toward the summit of Mount Bidwell, right near the place where California and Nevada come together at the Oregon border. We topped out over a break called Fandango Pass.

The pass was named by wagon-train parties on the old Apple-gate cutoff to the gold country around Jacksonville. From that height they got their first glimpse of Oregon, and they camped on the summit and danced themselves some fandangos, whatever the step might be.

And we, in our ranch-boy style, did some dancing of our own. Who knows how it started, but with linked arms and hands we stumbled and skipped through the last shards of night and into the sunrise. Still drunk, I fell and bloodied my hands and stood breathing deep of the morning air and sucking at my own salty blood, shivering and pissing and watching the stunted fir and meadow aspen around me come luminous with light, and I knew our night of traveling had brought me to this happiness that would never bear talking about. No more nameless sorrow, not with these comrades, and we all knew it and remained silent.

Seventeen. I was safe forever, and I could see 70 miles out across the beauty of country where I would always live with these friends, all of it glowing with morning.

We LEARN IT early in the West, drinking and driving, chasing away from the ticking stillness of home toward some dim aura glowing over the horizon, call it possibility or excitement. Henry James once said there are two mental states, excitement and lack of excitement, and that unfortunately excitement was more interesting than lack of excitement. Travel the highways in Montana, and you will see little white crosses along the dangerous curves, marking places where travelers have died, many of them drunk, and most of them searching and unable to name what it was they were missing at home. It's like a sport; you learn techniques.

For instance, there are three ways to go: alone, with cronies of either sex, or with someone you cherish beyond all others at that particular moment. We'll call that one love and save it for last.

Although each of these modes can get tricky, alone is the most delicate to manage. Alone can lead to loneliness, and self-pity,

and paranoia, and things like that – the trip can break down
into dark questing after dubious companionship.

The advantage of going it alone lies, of course, in spontaneity
and freedom. You don't have to consult anybody but your in-
clinations. You touch that warm car, and you climb in for a moment and roll down the window, just to see what it would be like.

And then, it's magic – you're rolling, you're gone and you're
riding. Shit fire, you think, they don't need me, not today. I'm
sick. This is sick leave. You know it's true. You've been sick, and
this day of freedom will cure your great illness. Adios.

Say it is spring, as in *to rise or leap suddenly and swiftly*, the most
dangerous and frothy season, sap rising and the wild geese
honking as they fly off toward the north. "Ensnared with flowers, I fall on grass." Andrew Marvell.

It might be the first day of everything, in which we rediscover
a foreverland of freedom and beauty before the invention of
guilt. A day when the beasts will all lie down with one another.
Hummingbirds in the purple lilac.

What we are talking about is the first day of high and classical
spring here in the temperate zones, one of those pure and art-
less mornings somewhere toward the latter part of May or early
June in the countries where I have lived, when the cottonwood
leaves have sprung from the bud and stand young and pale
green against the faint, elegant cleanliness of the sky. We are
talking about walking outside into such a morning and breathing deeply.

Where I like to head out of Missoula is upstream along the
Blackfoot River, the asphalt weaving and dipping and the
morning light lime-colored through the new leaves on the
aspen, with some fine, thin, fragile music cutting out from the
tape deck, perhaps Vivaldi concerti played on the cello. Such
music is important in the early day. It leaves a taste as clean as
the air across the mountain pastures, and it doesn't encourage
you to think. Later, there will be plenty of thinking.

But early on all I need is the music, and the motion of going, and some restraint. It always seems like a good idea, those

mornings up along the Blackfoot, to stop at Trixie's Antler Inn just as the doors are being unlocked. One drink for the road and some banter with the hippie girl tending bar.

But wrong.

After the first hesitation, more stopping at other such establishments is inevitable. And quite enjoyable, one after another. The Wheel Inn on the near outskirts of Lincoln, Bowmans Corner over south of Augusta, with the front of the Rockies rearing on the western skyline like purity personified.

Soon that fine blue bowl of heaven and your exquisite freedom are forgotten, and you are talking to strangers and to yourself. No more Vivaldi. It's only noon, and you are playing Hank Williams tapes and singing along, wondering if you could have made it in the country music business. By now you are a long and dangerous way from home and somewhat disoriented. The bartenders are studying you like a serious problem.

You have drifted into another mythology, called lonesome traveling and lost highways, a place where you really don't want to be on such a fine spring day. Once, it seemed like pure release to learn that you could vote with your feet, that you could just walk away like a movie star. Or, better yet, load your gear in some old beater pickup truck and drive. Half an hour, the vainglorious saying went, and I can have everything on rubber. Half an hour, and I'll be rolling. You just watch, little darling.

For some of us, the consequences of such escape tended to involve sitting alone with a pint bottle of whiskey in some ancient motel room where the television didn't work. The concept was grand and theatrical, but doing it, getting away, was oftentimes an emotional rat's nest of rootlessness. Country music, all that worn-out drifter syncopation, turned out to be another lie, a terrific sport but a real thin way of life.

So, some rules for going alone: Forget destinations; go where you will, always planning to stay overnight. Stop at historical markers, and mull over the ironies of destiny as you drive on. By now you are listening to bluegrass, maybe a tape from a Seldom Seen concert. And you are experiencing no despair.

Think of elk in the draws, buffalo on the plains, and the complex precision of predator-prey relationships. Be interesting, and love your own company. There is no need to get drunk and kill somebody on the road. Quite soon enough it will be twilight, and you can stop in some little town, check in at one of the two motels along the river, amble down to the tavern, and make some new friends. Such a pretty life.

TRAVELING WITH CRONIES is another matter. Some obvious organizational efforts are implicit. There stands your beloved car, warm in the sun. You touch a fender and turn away and backtrack toward your telephone, which magically starts ringing. Others have the same idea. My rig, your ice chest, bring money, we're traveling.

But the real logistical niceties lie in the chemistry of compatibility. Not just every good friend is a fit companion for the heedless expeditions of a summer drive. Each stop and turnoff must seem the result of consultation with mutual inclination. Nothing spoils traveling more quickly than endless debate, or any debate at all. Trust the driver. Everybody knows what we're looking for. Take us there.

Which is where? Looking for what? Call it ineffable – that which cannot be expressed or described and is not to be spoken of. Traveling with cronies can't be heedless without unspoken agreement.

Back when we were young and idiot, we would head up to The Stockman's in Arlee, hit the Buffalo Park in Ravali, move on to the 44 Bar north of St. Ignatius, and then make the Charlo turn to Tiny's. From there whim led the way until we ended up in the Eastgate Lounge in Missoula around midnight. The circuit was called The Inner Circle.

Say the afternoon sky is streaked white, and spring winds drive storm clouds over the peaks of Montana's Mission Mountains. This is the Flathead Valley, and the town is Charlo, and though it may seem impersonal now, it need not be. If you are in any way sensible, your next move should be simple and clear and rewarding. You and your companions will clump down the stairs and into Tiny's Tavern. The place used to be called Tiny's Blind Pig, *blind pig* being prohibition code for tavern. The old name, for those of us who stopped by when we were passing through, implied a connection with the romance we were seeking – an outlaw dream of prohibition, dusty black automobiles just in from a rum-run to Canada, blonde gum-snapping molls. As newcomers we ached to be a part of Montana – and here it was, the real goddamned item.

One night my brother was shooting pool at Tiny's with a wiry old man, an electrician by trade as I recall. During a lull in the bar talk I heard something that stood the hair on the back of my neck. "Son of a bitch," my brother said, "I wouldn't have to cheat to beat you."

Oh, pray for us, Lord. Outlanders in a bar filled with local ranchers and their brawny sons celebrating another victory for the best eight-man football team in the history of Montana. Do not let them beat on us – at least, not on me. Take my brother.

The rancher next to me, about a foot taller than I will ever be, looked sideways and grinned. "Don't know about you," he said, "but I ain't going over there. Them old black eyes take about three weeks to heal." By the time I had bought him and me a drink, my brother and the electrician were finishing their game without any further hint of warfare.

Well, I thought, got myself home again. Home is a notion such backcountry taverns seem to radiate – at least if they're places that long-time patrons and their barkeep hosts have imprinted with the wear and damage of their personalities. Tiny's was shaped as much as anything by the old man who owned it when I first went there – ancient and hurting, hobbling around on crutches, a former police chief from Miami, Florida, with a

huge collection of memorabilia in glass cases around the bar —
over 5000 different kinds of beer bottle, intimate snapshots of
Hitler taken in the 1930s, fine obsidian arrowheads, gem-
quality Kennedy half-dollars. Tiny is dead now, and they've
changed the sign over the doorway. But his collections are still
in place.

Homes and love, if they are to exist as more than fond children of the imagination, most often take us by surprise on back
roads. On my way to Missoula almost every day I pass the old
Milltown Union Bar, where Dick Hugo used to do his main
drinking in the days when he was serious about it. Above the
doorway white heads of mountain goat and bighorn sheep,
sealed in plexiglass bubbles, contemplate those who enter. As
Hugo said in a poem about the Milltown, "You were nothing going in, and now you kiss your hand." In another poem, about
another barroom, Hugo named the sense of recognition and
homecoming I expect upon going into one of the taverns I love.
His poem begins, "Home. Home. I knew it entering."

INDEED, WHAT are we looking for? In July of 1969 I came to
Montana to stay, bearing a new Master of Fine Arts degree
from the flooding heartland of Iowa. I had just finished up as
a thirty-five-year-old, in-off-the-ranch graduate student in the
Iowa Writer's Workshop, and I had lucked into a teaching job
at the University of Montana. I was running to native cover in
the west; I was a certified writer, and this was the beginning of
my real life at last.

During that summer in Iowa City — drinking too much, in
love with theories about heedlessness and possibility — I was trying to figure out how to inhabit my daydream. We lived in an old
stone-walled house with a flooded basement out by the Coral-
ville reservoir, listening to cockroaches run on the nighttime
lineoleum and imagining Montana, where we would find a
home.

Every morning the corn in the fields across the road looked

to have grown six inches, every afternoon the skies turned green with tornado-warning storms, and every night lightning ran magnificent and terrible from the horizons. My wife said they ought to build a dike around the whole damned state of Iowa and turn it into a catfish preserve. The U-Haul trailer was loaded. After a last party we were history in the Midwest, gone to Montana, where we were going to glow in the dark.

The real West started at the long symbolic interstate bridge over that mainline to so many ultimately heart-breaking American versions of heaven, the Missouri River. Out in the middle of South Dakota I felt myself released into significance. It was clear I was aiming my life in the correct direction. We were headed for a town studded with abandoned tipi burners.

But more so – as we drove I imagined Lewis and Clark and Catlin and Bodmer and even Audubon up to Fort Union on the last voyage of his life in 1843, along with every wagon train, ox-cart, cattle drive, and trainload of honyockers, all in pursuit of that absolute good luck which is some breathing time in a commodious place where the best that can be is right now. In the picture book of my imagination I was seeing a Montana composed of major post cards. The great river sliding by under the bridge was rich with water from the Sun River drainage, where elk and grizzly were rumored to be on the increase.

Engrossed in fantasies of traveling upriver into untouched territory, I was trying to see the world fresh, as others had seen it. On April 22, 1805, near what is now the little city of Williston in North Dakota, Meriwether Lewis wrote:

> ...immense herds of buffalo, elk, deer, and antelopes feeding in one common and boundless pasture. We saw a large number of beaver feeding on the bark of trees along the verge of the river, several of which we shot. Found them large and fat.

By 1832, at the confluence of the Missouri and the Yellowstone, the painter George Catlin was already tasting ashes while

trying to envision a future – just as I was trying to imagine what
had been seen. Catlin wrote:

> ...the native Indian in his classic attire, galloping his wild
> horse, with sinewy bow, and shield and lance, amid the fleet-
> ing herds of elks and buffaloes. What a beautiful and thrilling
> specimen for America to preserve and hold up to the view of
> her refined citizens and the world, in future ages! A *nation's
> park*, containing man and beast, in all the wild and freshness
> of their nature's beauty!

Think of Audubon responding eleven years later, on May 17,
1843, in that same upriver country around Fort Union:

> Ah! Mr. Catlin, I am now sorry to see and to read your
> accounts of the Indians you saw – how very different they
> must have been from any that I have seen!

On July 21, Audubon writes:

> What a terrible destruction of life, as it were for nothing,
> or next to it, as the tongues only were brought in, and the
> flesh of these fine animals were left to beasts and birds of
> prey, or to rot on the spots where they fell. The prairies were
> literally covered with the skulls of victims.

On August 5 Audubon finishes the thought:

> But this cannot last; even now there is a perceptible differ-
> ence in the size of the herds, and before many years the
> Buffalo, like the Great Auk, will have disappeared; surely this
> should not be permitted.

In our summer of 1969 we poked along the edge where the
Badlands break so suddenly from the sunbaked prairies, imagining the faraway drumming of hooves, Catlin's warriors on
their decorated horses coming after us from somewhere out of
dream. Not so far south lay Wounded Knee.

We studied the stone faces of our forefathers at Mount Rushmore and didn't see a damned thing because by that time in the afternoon we were blinded by so much irony on a single day. We retired for the night to a motel somewhere south of the Devil's Post Pile in Wyoming. I was seeing freshly, but not always what I hoped to see. The distances were terrifying.

By the time we reached Missoula, I had disassociated my sensibilities with whiskey, which gave me the courage to march up the concrete steps to Richard Hugo's house, only a block from the Clark Fork River, where the Village Inn Motel sits these days. I rapped on his door. He studied me a moment after I introduced myself. "You're very drunk," he said.

Well hell, I thought, now you've done it.

"Wait a minute," Hugo said. "I'll join you."

Home, I thought, childlike with relief. This was the new country I had been yearning for, inhabited by this man who smiled and seemed to think I should be whatever I could manage.

I was lucky to know Dick Hugo, and his collected poems, *Making Sure It Goes On*, heads my list of good books written about the part of the world where I live. Dick loved to drive Montana, his trips imaginative explorations into other lives as a way toward focusing on his own complexities. He made the game of seeing into art, and his poetry and life form a story that lies rock bottom in my understanding of what art is for.

Once we drove over to fish the Jefferson River on a summer day when we were both hung-over to the point of insipid visionary craziness. We didn't catch any fish, and I came home numb, simply spooked, but Dick saw some things, and wrote a poem:

SILVER STAR

> This is the final resting place of engines,
> farm equipment and that rare, never more

than occasional man. Population:
17. Altitude unknown. For no
good reason you can guess, the woman
in the local store is kind. Old steam trains
have been rusting here so long, you feel
the urge to oil them, to lay new track, to start
the west again. The Jefferson
drifts by in no great hurry on its way
to wed the Madison, to be a tributary
to the ultimately dirty brown Missouri.
This town supports your need to run alone.

What if you'd lived here young, gone full of fear
to that stark brick school, the cruel teacher
supported by your guardian? Think well
of the day you ran away to Whitehall.
Think evil of the cop who found you starving
and returned you, siren open, to the house
you cannot find today. The answer comes back wrong.
There was no house. They never heard your name.

When you leave, leave in a flashy car
and wave goodbye. You are a stranger
every day. Let the engines and the farm
equipment die, and know that rivers
end and never end, lose and never lose
their famous names. What if your first girl
ended certain she was animal, barking
at the aides and licking floors? You know
you have no answers. The empty school
burns red in heavy snow.

Each time I read "Silver Star" I rediscover a story about
homes, and the courage to acknowledge such a need, a story
about Dick and his continual refinding of his own life, and an
instruction about storytelling as the art of constructing road
maps, ways home to that ultimate shelter which is the coherent
self. Montana is a landscape reeking with such conjunction and
resonance. They fill the silence.

Not long ago, on a bright spring morning, I stood on the cliffs of the Ulm Pishkun where the Blackfeet drove dusty hundreds of bison to fall and die. Gazing east I could dimly see the great Anaconda Company smokestack there on the banks of the Missouri like a finger pointing to heaven above the old saloon-town city of Great Falls where Charlie Russell painted and traded his pictures for whiskey – only a little upstream from the place where Meriwether Lewis wrote, having just finished an attempt at describing his first sight of the falls:

> After writing this imperfect description, I again viewed the falls, and was so much disgusted with the imperfect idea it conveyed of the scene, that I determined to draw my pen across it and begin again; but then reflected that I could not perhaps succeed better....

After so many months of precise notation, all in the service of Thomas Jefferson's notion of the West as useful, in one of the most revealing passages written about the American West, Lewis seems to be saying:

> But this, this otherness is beyond the capture of my words, this cannot be useful, this is dream.

The dam-builders, of course, did not see it his way.

Behind me loomed the fortress of the rock-sided butte Charlie Russell painted as backdrop to so much history, with the Rockies off beyond on the western horizon, snowy and gleaming in the morning sun. This listing could go on, but I was alone and almost frightened by so many conjunctions visible at once, and so many others right down the road: the Gates of the Mountains and Last Chance Gulch and even make-believe – Boone Caudill and Teal Eye and Dick Summers over west on the banks of the Teton River, where it cuts through the landscapes of *The Big Sky* – history evident all around and the imaginings of artists and storytellers intertwined. Charlie Russell and Bud Guthrie and Dick Hugo and Meriwether Lewis created metaphoric territory as real as any other Montana in the eye of my imagination.

We all play at transporting ourselves new into new country, seeing freshly, reorienting ourselves and our schemes within the complexities of the world. It is a powerful connection to history, and the grand use we make of storytelling as we incessantly attempt to recognize that which is sacred and the point of things.

WHICH BRINGS US to our most complex option, traveling with lovers. In Missoula, in the heart of winter, if you are me, you talk in a placating way to the woman you love. It is about three days after you forgot another country custom, *The Valentine Party.* You suggest ways of redeeming yourself. You talk to friends. An expedition forms.

This paragon of a woman owns an aging four-wheel-drive Chevrolet pickup, three-quarter-ton, and she and I and her twin boys set off in that vehicle. Only praying a little bit. Good rubber, but a clanking U-joint. The friends – a southern California surfer hooked on snow skiing of all varieties, and a lady of his acquaintance – set off in that lady's vintage Volvo. We also pray for them. The Volvo wanders in its steering, in a somewhat experimental way. But no need for real fear. These are Montana highways.

Out of Missoula we caravan south through the Bitterroot Valley, where – before the subdivisions – Tom Jefferson could have seen his vision of pastoral American happiness realized. The Volvo wanders, the U-joint clanks, and we are happy. We wind up over Lost Trail Pass, where Lewis and Clark experienced such desperate vertigo in the wilderness on their way west. At the summit we turn east, toward the Big Hole Basin and a town named Wisdom. At 6,000 feet, the altitude in the Big Hole is too much for deciduous trees. The only color is the willow along the creeks, the red of dried blood.

We pass the Big Hole Battlefield, where Joseph and Looking Glass and the Nez Percés suffered ambush by Federal troops under General Oliver Otis Howard on the morning of August 11, 1877. Casualties: Army, 29 killed, 40 wounded; Nez Percé, by Army body count, 89 dead, most of them women and children. We are traveling through the rich history of America.

Winter has come down on this country like a hammer, but the defroster is working perfectly and there is a bar in Wisdom with dozens of stuffed birds and animals on display around the walls. The place is crowded with weekend snowmobile fans in their bright insulated nylon coveralls. There is a stuffed quail on a stand with its head torn off. All that's left is just a little wire sticking out of the neck. What fun that night must have been.

The bar is fine. No one cares when we bring in our own cheeses and stoneground wheat crackers. We slice on the bar top, scatter crumbs. The bartender cleans up our mess. Smiles. The kids play the pinball machine all they want. We have hot drinks. So we are slightly tipsy, not to say on the verge of drunk, when we line out south toward Jackson. This is the deep countryside of Montana, and no one cares. The Volvo doesn't wander as erratically. The U-joint has made peace with itself. Which is something country people know about mechanical devices. They oftentimes heal. At least for a little while.

The Big Hole is called the "Land of 10,000 Haystacks." Nearby, a country man is feeding his cattle. Pitching hay with ice in his mustache. He has been doing it every day for two months. He has a month to go. Feeding cattle never was any fun. We do not think about such matters.

Beyond Polaris we head up a canyon between five-foot banks of snow, and we are arrived. Elkhorn Hot Springs. Right away, we like it. Snowshoeing and cross-country in all directions, and for our surfer friend, a dandy little downhill area only about three miles away. We have a cabin with a fireplace that works fine after the wood dries out. Up in the lodge they are serving family-style dinners. And cheap. You know — roast beef and meat loaf and real mashed potatoes and creamed corn and pickled beets. And on and on. Maybe this is the moment to break out the bottle of rum.

Eventually we wander down to the hot baths, the indoor sauna pools and the outdoor pool, and the snow falling into our mouths. Snowball fights in the water. Rowdiness. Young boys in swimming suits created from cut-off Levis. And the next day, sweet red wine in the snow and white chilled wine in the evening, and the ache from all the skiing melting out of our knees into the hot water.

But electricity is in fact the way nature behaves. Nothing lasts. That was winters ago. My surfer friend went off hunting the last good wave. He wrote from Australia, extolling the virtues of the unexamined life. The Volvo is dead; the U-joint is fixed. Desire and pursuit of the whole is called love.

CONTRIBUTORS

JOHN BERGER'S most recent book is *The Sense of Sight*. He is a contributing editor of *The Threepenny Review*, where "Her Secrets" was first published.

TERRENCE DES PRES publishes his essays widely. His book, *The Survivor: An Anatomy of Life in the Death Camps*, is published by Oxford University Press. He teaches at Colgate University in Hamilton, New York.

ANNIE DILLARD'S essays on nature and the spirit are well-known. Her most recent book is *Encounters with Chinese Writers*.

GRETEL EHRLICH'S *The Solace of Open Spaces* was published in 1985. She lives in Wyoming.

JAMES FENTON writes drama reviews for *The Times of London*, and his poetry is published widely in England and in the United States. His book of poems is *Children in Exile*. "The Snap Election" is the first part of a three-part article that was published in *Granta*.

RICHARD FORD'S collection of short stories will be published early in 1987. His most recent book is his novel, *The Sportswriter*. He recently moved from Mississippi to Missoula, Montana.

JOHN HAINES is best known for his poetry – most recently his selected poems, *News from the Glacier*. He spent nearly twenty years homesteading in Alaska and now lives near Fairbanks.

PATRICIA HAMPL is the author of the memoir, *A Romantic Education*, as well as two volumes of poems. In April 1987, Milkweed Editions will publish *Spillville*, with prose text by her and engravings by Steven Sorman. The piece published here is chapter one of a memoir about Catholic girlhood with reflections on contemplative life, a work in progress.

WILLIAM KITTREDGE's *We Are Not in This Together*, a collection of short stories, was published by Graywolf Press in 1984. His essays have appeared in *Rocky Mountain News*, *Outside*, and other magazines. They will appear together as a Graywolf book in Spring 1987.

BARRY LOPEZ and his most recent book, *Arctic Dreams*, have been blessed with praise for the book's evocation of the natural life of the Arctic. He lives on the McKenzie River, an hour from Eugene, Oregon.

PHILLIP MOFFITT is Editor in Chief and President of *Esquire*. His essays appear regularly in the magazine's "Backstage at Esquire" column.

SUZANNAH LESSARD is a staff writer at *The New Yorker*.

BRENDA PETERSON's novel *River of Light* has recently been published in paperback by Graywolf Press. She works as an environmental writer in Seattle.

DAVID QUAMMEN has a monthly column in *Outside* magazine. His essays on science have been gathered into a book, *Natural Acts*, and he is the author of a mystery novel and of a book of three novellas to be published by Graywolf Press.